MW00568205

SCENTS OF MEMORY

SCENTS OF MEMORY

A delightful mix of stories
and delicious recipes from around the world

Souad Sharabani

Published by Voice Print Educational Productions
copyright © 2014 Souad Sharabani
All photography copyright © as listed below

All rights reserved. No part of this publication, including text and photographs, may be reproduced, modified, copied or transmitted in any form or by any means, or used for any commercial purpose, without the prior written permission of the author.

"The Horse," which appears on page 34, is reproduced by kind permission of Zakaria Mohammed.

LIBRARY AND ARCHIVES CANADA CATALOGUING IN PUBLICATION

Sharabani, Souad, 1950-, author
    Scents of memory : a delightful mix of stories and delicious recipes from around the world / Souad Sharabani.

Issued in print and electronic formats.
ISBN 9780991866113 (pod).— ISBN 978-0-9918661-0-6 (pdf).
ISBN 978-09918661-2-0 (ebook)

    1. Cooking, Middle Eastern. 2. Cooking.
3. Sharabani, Souad, 1950- --Travel. 4. Cookbooks. I. Title.

TX725.M628S53 2014   641.5956   C2013-900806-3
                                        C2014-900843-0

Front cover: Sweet-and-Sour Apricot Stew, page 86
Cover and food photography: Cori Chong © 2014
Editing: Judy Phillips
Design and production: Peter Ross / Counterpunch Inc

To order copies of this book, visit www.scentsofmemory.com

To my family

CONTENTS

INTRODUCTION
FOOD AND MEMORIES

Cooking and eating are interwoven with my life experiences and memories. They are not simply necessities to feed the body. Although I do not have a collection of cookbooks in my kitchen, I do have a collection of vivid memories from childhood, from travelling, from work, and of the people I've met or grew up with. My memories of incidents are always combined with and connected to those of certain dishes. And I love to tell stories and to cook; in fact, there is a unique connection at a very basic, universal level between the recipes and the stories; between receiving and giving, between biology and psychology. Over the years, as I became more comfortable in my own skin, the memories came back to me and my desire to cook grew stronger.

I learned or remembered the tastes of most of the dishes described in this book by remembering their aromas. I recall being in Egypt and walking into a spice store in a local market. It was a trip down memory lane. With my eyes closed, I smelled the spices, running them through my fingers, remembering in which dish I had this one or that one. It is almost eerie how now I am able to cook a dish I had just by remembering its scent. The first time I decided to cook *qormeh sabzi*—beef and spinach stew and herbs—a dish I ate often as a kid, I went to the grocery store and sniffed various herbs to refresh my memory of the aromas and flavours of the dish. Then I went home and made it from scratch. It turned out perfectly.

My life and work has taken me to five continents, where I have had experiences worlds apart from each other. The stories that come from them are often extraordinary, and it is my privilege to share them with you.

THE RECIPES

My recipes are predominantly Middle Eastern in origin, with others from Latin America and North America, Asia and Africa. In almost all I've altered the ingredients somewhat from the traditional recipes to reflect the flavours that have evolved in my version of these dishes over the years.

Growing up, I ate mostly vegetable and legume stews, with little meat or poultry. They were not complicated or expensive dishes, but, made with a mix of herbs and spices, they were always full of flavour. Later, my travel and work around the world often entailed living and eating among some of the most disenfranchised

With children at a Calcutta orphanage, 1998

people in society; the food I ate on those trips were also mainly vegetable and legume dishes—affordable dishes aimed at feeding the people cheaply. But they, too, were full of flavour.

Although my recipes, based on these foods and dishes, are linked to my stories, neither is presented chronologically. Instead, the recipes are grouped by type of dish—dips, salads, soups, main courses and desserts—to help you plan your menu. But you'll also find, at the back of the book, the recipes listed according to the main ingredient. Since the recipes are based on the way my family cooked when I was growing up and the way I ate while living in Africa, Asia and Latin America, they are predominantly for vegetable stews with lots of herbs and spices and a little bit of meat or poultry added—chickpea stew with cinnamon and allspice; celery stew with lemon and mint; spinach with lentils, mint and lemon; tomato soup with zucchini and basil; creamy squash soup with curry and coriander. In fact, when I go grocery shopping, I do not think about how much meat and poultry I need; I think about what vegetable dish I'll prepare: celery, spinach or perhaps an okra dish. So it's only natural that I followed this tradition when writing this cookbook.

The recipes in this book are healthy, tasty, easy to find ingredients for, simple and inexpensive to make. With these recipes, you can feed four to six or more people for less than ten dollars. The recipes can easily be doubled or tripled to feed a larger gathering. In fact, in the last few years, I have cooked on a volunteer basis once a week for up to 140 homeless people. I am honoured to see them thoroughly enjoying the meals, made from recipes included in this book. I am also pleased to have been able to cook for so many people on a very limited budget—typically I have no more than $140 to spend on ingredients. So when I cook such a massive quantity, I simply adjust the amount of vegetables or add other vegetables as well, use less meat and slightly modify the spices—and still come out with beautiful results.

Rice fields, Nepal, 1998

Starters are part and parcel of Middle Eastern cooking and culture. When Palestinians, Lebanese or Egyptians sit down for a snack, a meal or even just a drink, the table is always filled with starters, from tahini, babaganoush and labne to cut vegetables, pickles and pita. As long as someone is sitting at a table, they are guaranteed to be served starters. Starters remain on the table even once the main courses are served. Here are a few recipes I think you will enjoy.

STARTERS

Labne (background); Chickpeas with Tahini (centre);
Roasted Eggplant with Tahini and Lemon (foreground)

SESAME SEED BUTTER
TAHINI

Makes about ½ cup

¼ cup water
4 Tbsp tahini paste
juice of 1 lemon
2 cloves garlic
3 Tbsp chopped parsley
1 Tbsp cumin
½ Tbsp chili flakes (optional)
salt and pepper

The first time I was invited for dinner in a Palestinian home, there was a buffet with at least a dozen dishes. I was quite intrigued by the number of dishes that were served with tahini or *rashi* (sesame seed butter), as it is called in Arabic: *hummus bel tahini*—eggplants with tahini, or babaganoush; on falafel; on *kubbe*—spiced meatballs; on stuffed zucchini; on salads and in desserts—molasses or date syrup with tahini. The hostess sensed I was not used to that much tahini, and said, "Well, Souad, welcome to a Palestinian home; tahini is as much a part of our staple diet as za'atar and olive oil. It is rich, but it sure tastes good." I'd have to agree with her.

1. Put all ingredients in a food processor and blend until smooth. To thin, add a little bit of water or lemon juice. To thicken, just add another spoonful of tahini.

HOMEMADE YOGURT

Makes about 9 cups

16 cups 2% milk
1 cup skim-milk powder
6 oz 3.5% plain yogurt

I started to make yogurt a few years back. Homemade is much less expensive than store-bought, the cost of which adds up if you eat a lot of it, like I do. I use this yogurt to make labne (page 16); this amount lasts my family of four for two weeks, eating it almost every day for breakfast. You can also use this yogurt for any of the recipes calling for plain yogurt.

1. In a heavy-bottomed large pot, combine the milk and skim-milk powder. Heat until scalding, at 180°F to 185°F, stirring continuously to prevent burning.
2. Remove from the heat and let cool slightly. (To cool the milk faster, place the pot in the sink, adding enough cold water to the sink to come halfway up the pot.) Once the milk has cooled to 130°F, transfer to a big bowl.
3. Put the yogurt in a small bowl. Add 5 to 6 Tbsp of the warm milk and mix well. Pour the yogurt mixture into the remaining warm milk, stirring very gently.
4. Cover the bowl with a lid, towel or even a small blanket and set in a warm place. (I sometimes put it in the oven overnight with the light on, or in the microwave to sit.) Once you set it down, do not move it for at least 8 hours.
5. Then chill the yogurt in the refrigerator for at least 4 hours before serving.

YOGURT CUCUMBER DIP

At Montreal's McGill Library, where I worked even though I was semi-illiterate, I made friends with some students who also worked there. One invited me to her wedding shower. Traditionally in the Middle East, on the night before a woman's wedding, she goes to the public bath to wash and purify herself before her wedding night. So when the young woman invited me to her "shower," I thought we were going to a public bath.

I arrived at the girl's middle-class home, my bar of soap and sponge in a paper bag—what else did I need? The hostess welcomed me, took my coat, then asked if I had brought anything. Very softly I said yes. She asked me to put it on the table in the living room. "No, it is okay, I will hold on to my bag," I said, not understanding why she wanted me to put it on the table. But she insisted, so I hesitantly went into the living room, where I saw a table piled with gifts. I immediately realized something was wrong.

"Just put it on the table," the hostess repeated. I did what I was told and joined the others for supper, starting to feel self-conscious. I took a plate and filled it with all the goodies, including a tangy cucumber dip. A while later, the hostess called us to the living room and asked us to sit in a circle so she could begin opening the presents. I tried to leave but was cornered by my friend, who pleaded with me to stay a bit longer. I took a chair by the door, feeling sick. With what seemed like the tips of her fingers, my friend picked up the paper bag and took out my old soap and sponge. There was silence in the room. No one laughed or made even a noise. With my head down, I got up and left the house as fast as I could. I knew there was no point in explaining.

◈ ◈ ◈

1. In a bowl, mix the yogurt with the cucumber and mint.
2. Combine the dressing ingredients and stir into the yogurt mixture.

VARIATION
For a thick drink, add 2 cups chopped ice.

Serves 6

2 cups homemade yogurt
    (page 14) or labne (page 16)
½ English cucumber,
    very finely chopped
2 Tbsp dried mint

Dressing
3 Tbsp olive oil
dash of lemon juice
2 cloves garlic, crushed,
    with a pinch of salt
¼ tsp pepper
salt

LABNE

Makes about 6 cups

3 cups 3.5% or plain yogurt,
or homemade yogurt
(page 14)

Labne is basically drained yogurt. My family eats labne for breakfast with jam or with mixed vegetables, za'atar, olives and pickles, or as a dip. Sprinkled with a little olive oil and stored in an airtight container in the refrigerator, it will last more than 2 weeks.

◈   ◈   ◈

1. Pour unstirred yogurt into a large square of cheesecloth. Tie the four corners together to make a bundle and place in a strainer.
2. Let the yogurt drain into a bowl, in the refrigerator, for 24 hours. The longer it drains, the firmer it becomes.

LABNE DIP

Serves 4 to 6

½ cup labne
3 Tbsp olive oil
2 Tbsp za'atar

The rule of thumb in Arabic families is that no matter how poor you are, you offer everything you can to make a guest welcome in your home. I once visited a poor Palestinian family with ten or twelve children, to interview the parents for a documentary. As soon as I arrived at their home, the mother brought out fresh bread, cut vegetables, olives and, of course, labne and za'atar. "Eat," she said. I would have offended her if I had not stuffed my face.

Za'atar, a mix of seasonings, usually thyme, sumac and roasted sesame seeds, is available at Middle Eastern, health food and fine food stores. Serve this dip with bread or sliced vegetables.

◈   ◈   ◈

1. In a bowl, combine all the ingredients.

SWEET PEPPER DIP

Serves 6 to 8

Years ago, my husband and I went to a Greek island for a vacation. We spent the days on the beach and in the evenings took a taxi through the narrow mountain roads to town. We hired the same taxi driver for the three weeks we were there because we liked him and he liked us, and we managed to communicate a little, even though we spoke different languages. On our last day we offered to take him and his family to dinner. He was very excited.

He picked us up in the taxi and, after a half-hour drive, stopped in front of a long, long flight of wide steps—there must have been hundreds of them. Houses sat on either side, giving the impression of being on a cliff. We started our climb up the steps, but there was no restaurant in sight. Eventually, we reached the top and there saw five or six tables positioned on the landing. Young kids were running about, and there was a long lineup of people waiting to be seated. They were all locals who had been coming to this restaurant for years.

The taxi driver took us into the kitchen—not much more than a small closet with three burners—to meet the owners. This gentle, soft-spoken couple in their mid-fifties cooked, served and cleaned. They made only appetizers, most consisting of seafood, salads and roasted vegetables, and the food was out of this world. We stayed at the restaurant for hours, managing to communicate with the taxi driver and his family using the little dictionary I had. At around midnight the owners joined us. Of course, they continued to bring us food. I loved every minute of that evening. And I would like to emulate here one of the dishes: sweet pepper dip.

◈   ◈   ◈

5 sweet peppers (combination of red, yellow and orange), quartered

1½ pitas or 8 slices baguette

juice of ½ lemon

3 cloves garlic

½ cup chopped black or green olives

½ cup chopped fresh basil or parsley

5 Tbsp olive oil

1 Tbsp dried oregano

½ tsp pepper or chopped jalapeño pepper (remove seeds for less heat)

salt

1. Roast the peppers in a 425°F oven or on the barbecue for 15 minutes per side or until charred.
2. Toast the bread until crispy.
3. Place the peppers and remaining ingredients, including the toasted bread, in a food processor and pulse for a few minutes.
4. Adjust the salt, pepper, lemon and herbs to taste. The dip should have a subtle lemon flavour.

ROASTED EGGPLANT WITH TAHINI AND LEMON
BABAGANOUSH

Serves 4 to 6

1 eggplant

½ bunch green onions, chopped

1 roasted pepper (optional)

1 tomato (optional)

3 cloves garlic, chopped

juice of 1 lemon

¼ cup chopped parsley

3 Tbsp olive oil

2 Tbsp tahini paste

1 Tbsp cumin

1 tsp pepper

salt

Variation 2:
Mild Babaganoush

1 eggplant

8 fresh mint leaves, chopped

2 cloves garlic, chopped

2 roasted green or red peppers

½ cup chopped parsley

4 Tbsp olive oil

3 Tbsp white wine vinegar or
    juice of ½ lemon

1½ Tbsp cumin

2 tsp pepper

salt

Years ago I worked with a student named Asher at McGill Library in Montreal. His goals in life were to persuade me to join a union and to teach me how to distinguish between different "white people" because, as an Arab woman, I could not tell the difference.

There was a woman who came every day to borrow books, yet none of us behind the desk had warmed to her; she struck us as a know-it-all. One day while Asher and I were talking about babaganoush, she interrupted us to say we were wrong about the ingredients. You can understand that I did not take this lightly. One of the few things I knew about, she was trying to own.

Ten years later, in Toronto, I bumped into this woman on the street. She said, "Hi, you are Shoshana, aren't you?" calling me by my Hebrew name. I said no and continued walking. I just could not bear talking to her. For weeks and months afterward, I kept bumping into her, and she would say "You are Shoshana," and I would say "No, you are mistaken" and keep walking.

The grand finale took place one day at the gym. I was in the shower washing my hair when the curtains were suddenly yanked open. And there she was, screaming, "You are Shoshana, aren't you?" I did not know which part of my body to cover, and the shampoo was getting into my eyes and blinding me. Like a dog with its tail between its legs, I said, "Yep, it is me."

She yelled, "You idiot!" and walked away, not even closing the curtains. Maybe I am an idiot, but an idiot who knows how to make babaganoush.

This is a very easy dip to make.

◈ ◈ ◈

1. Using a fork, prick the eggplant in several spots. Bake on a baking sheet or on the barbecue at 400°F for 30 to 35 minutes or until it is very tender—once the skin is squishy and peels off easily. Remove from the oven and let cool.
2. Peel the eggplant (or leave the skin on for a stronger flavour, just trim the stem) and transfer the flesh to a food processor. Add the remaining ingredients and process until smooth.
3. Adjust spices to taste. If it is too lemony, add a little more oil or tahini paste. If it needs more lemon, salt or pepper, add a little at a time.

VARIATION 1: ROASTED EGGPLANT SALAD
Instead of blending, chop the ingredients in a food processor.

VARIATION 2: MILD BABAGANOUSH
Prepare as directed in recipe.

CHICKPEAS WITH TAHINI
HUMMUS BEL TAHINI

When I was growing up in Israel, once a month my family would go to a local café to listen to Umm Kulthum, my parents' favourite singer, on the radio. To us, she was an Egyptian goddess, loved and admired throughout the Arab world. When she died, over four million people lined the streets of Cairo to say farewell. We went to the café because its radio had better signals than ours at home. It was also a way of connecting to people. I do not think there was a single Arab man or woman who did not listen to Umm Kulthum on those Thursday nights. The concerts would go on for hours, until the early hours of the morning. The orchestra played for at least two hours before Umm Kulthum started singing. And every man and woman in the café would sing along, or at least nod their heads to the music. I often saw women crying as they listened to the lyrics. We kids would be running around, eating, playing and, from time to time, falling asleep on the chairs. There was always a plate of *hummus bel tahini* to nibble on, along with a plate of cut vegetables and olives, not to mention *araak* (a liquor) and strong Arabic coffee.

To serve, sprinkle with olive oil and chili flakes, or garnish with parsley and a few olives. Accompany with pita bread.

1. In a food processor, purée the ingredients until very smooth. Taste occasionally, adding more seasonings and water as needed, a little at a time.
2. Pour the mixture into a deep bowl and serve.

Serves 6

1 can (19 oz/540 mL) chickpeas, drained and rinsed, or 2 cups cooked dried chickpeas (see page 156)

3 cloves garlic

juice of 1 lemon

4 Tbsp water

3 Tbsp tahini paste

2 Tbsp olive oil

2 tsp cumin

1 tsp pepper

salt

SPICED CHICKPEA TURNOVERS
SAMBUSAK BEL TAWA

Makes 20 to 30 turnovers

Dough

1 pkg (¼ oz/7 g) active dry yeast

1 Tbsp sugar

1 cup lukewarm water

3 cups whole-wheat flour (or equal parts whole-wheat and all-purpose)

1 tsp salt

Filling

1 to 2 cans (19 oz/540 mL each) chickpeas, drained and rinsed, or 2 to 4 cups cooked dried chickpeas (see page 156)

4 Tbsp oil

1 large onion, chopped

1 bunch green chopped onions

1 head garlic, chopped

1 cup chopped parsley

1 to 2 Tbsp cumin

1 to 2 Tbsp curry powder

1 Tbsp paprika

1 tsp turmeric

1 to 2 tsp pepper

salt

vegetable oil, for deep-frying

When I was growing up in the Middle East, most cooking was done in the early hours of the morning, at sunrise. Homes were not air-conditioned and it was usually too hot to cook indoors. As well, the main meal was at noon and often took hours to prepare. We cooked in large quantities, and every part of the meal was made from scratch and cooked on a little burner. Even the chickpeas or meat we ground by hand, with a *hawan,* or pestle and mortar. But all of it was done with great fun—neighbours and friends dropped by to talk and have a cup of tea.

Most Iraqi Jews make *sambusak bel tawa*—chickpeas in dough—during Purim, a Jewish holiday. I remember my aunt, my mother and a few friends and neighbours bent over little burners frying up a storm with all of us kids running around, eating the turnovers as they came out of the frying pans. To this day, I have no idea how those women were able to sit for hours bending down almost to the floor without hurting their legs or knees.

No matter where and how you cook them, these turnovers will taste scrumptious. Serve them as a starter or with a salad as a main. Cooked extras can be frozen in a flat container, layered between waxed paper.

NOTE: If you don't want to make the dough, use the smallest egg-roll wrappers you can find in the refrigerator section of the grocery store; you'll need 20 to 30 wrappers.

TO PREPARE THE DOUGH

1. In a large bowl, dissolve the yeast and sugar in the water. Set aside for 15 minutes.
2. Add the flour and salt to the yeast mixture and mix well to incorporate.
3. Turn the dough onto a lightly floured surface and knead until firm and elastic. If the dough is too dry, add more water, a little at a time.
4. Return the dough to the bowl, cover the bowl with a damp cloth and let the dough rise in a warm, draft-free place for about 2 hours.

TO PREPARE THE FILLING

1. In a food processor, purée the chickpeas.
2. In a large, deep frying pan, heat the oil and fry the onion, green onions and garlic until light golden.
3. Add the parsley and spices; cook for 2 to 4 minutes.
4. Remove from the heat, add the puréed chickpeas to the mixture, and stir to mix well. Taste and adjust the seasonings as needed—you should be able to taste the various spices.

1. *If using homemade dough,* roll the dough into small balls, then stretch each ball into a circle, about 3 inches in diameter, using your hands or a rolling pin. Spoon 1 to 2 Tbsp of the filling in the centre of a dough circle, fold the dough over and pinch tightly closed. The turnover will resemble a half-moon. Place on an ungreased baking sheet and, using a fork, press to flatten slightly.

2. *If using egg-roll wrappers,* spoon 1 to 2 Tbsp of the filling into the centre of each wrapper, fold and press closed on both ends, then roll into a cylinder shape. Place on an ungreased baking sheet.

3. Repeat with remaining dough and filling.

4. Heat the oil for deep-frying in a suitable pan over high heat. Using a spatula, very gently place the turnovers one by one in the pan, being careful not to overcrowd (cook in batches if necessary). Cook until light golden.

5. Remove with a slotted spoon and drain on paper towel. Transfer to a serving plate and serve hot.

BAKED EGGS
BETH AT BIT

Baked eggs are an integral part of almost every Iraqi family's Saturday morning ritual. To this day, my brother and his family eat this dish every weekend. It is delicious, especially when served with a garnish of fried or baked eggplant (page 55), pickle and salad.

1. Wrap eggs individually in foil.
2. Place directly on the centre oven rack and bake in a 325°F oven for 2 hours.

BAKED FIGS WITH CHEESE AND VINAIGRETTE

Figs are a delicate sweet fruit that grow in southern Europe, Asia and the Middle East. In much of North America, they are typically available only during the summer months. We either eat them plain or with walnuts. For a special occasion I bake them as a side dish.

1. On a baking sheet lined with parchment paper, spread out the figs. Place a slice of cheese on top of each.
2. Combine the vinegar, olive oil and spices.
3. With a teaspoon, sprinkle the cheese-topped figs with the vinegar mixture.
4. Bake in a 350°F oven for about 10 to 15 minutes or until the cheese is melted and the figs are warmed through.
5. Serve straight from the oven, while still warm.

Serves 4 to 6

8 to 10 figs, halved

8 to 10 small, thin slices mozzarella or other mild cheese

4 Tbsp balsamic vinegar

3 Tbsp olive oil

pinch each pepper, dried oregano and dried basil

Travelling and living in India, Nepal and China, I noticed that people there do not typically eat salads with their meals. Instead, they mix vegetables with legumes or poultry. The same goes for Iraqis: most times when Iraqis make stews, they do not make a salad to go with it. But when they prepare a strictly meat, chicken or fish dish, they do make a salad to accompany it.

On the other hand, throughout the Middle East, salads and cut raw vegetables are integral parts of every meal—including breakfast and snacks. Often breakfast consists of tomatoes, cucumber and olives, and bowls of labne (drained yogurt), olive oil and za'atar.

Salads do not need creamy dressings to make them delicious. For most of the salad recipes in this book, the dressing consists of fresh lemon juice and olive oil with garlic and onion. But there is lots of variety in the salads, from green salad to carrot salad, from tomato salad to cabbage salad to eggplant salad.

SALADS

Mango Salad

GREEN SALAD WITH LEMON GARLIC DRESSING

Serves 4 to 6

½ head Romaine lettuce, torn into bite-size pieces

1 tomato, chopped

¼ English cucumber, finely chopped

½ green or red pepper, finely chopped (optional)

¼ cup finely chopped Spanish or other sweet onion

Dressing

2 cloves garlic

pinch salt

3 Tbsp olive oil

juice of 1 lemon

1 tsp sumac (optional)

salt and pepper

I made a salad for a dinner party hosted by the woman I worked for in Neufchâtel, in Switzerland. On that day, I was very sick. My leg was badly infected—swollen, red and hot. I knew there was something very wrong with it, but I was an illegal, with no medical insurance. I was reluctant to tell my employer that I was sick, as I was afraid she might fire me. So I waited until I had a couple of hours off, took the money I had saved and went to see a doctor. He told me that I if I did not treat the infection right away, I would lose my leg. But I had only enough money to pay for the visit or for the medicine, not both. I sat on my knees, begging him to let me pay for the visit by joining the cleaning staff in his office on my free afternoons. He agreed.

I went back home as happy as a clown and had the energy to prepare dinner and serve the guests. I even wore uncomfortable high-heeled shoes and pantyhose that clung to my infected leg. After I had finished cleaning up, I took off my shoes and pantyhose and sat down on the kitchen floor with a bowl of this salad, dozing off as I ate.

Unlike the salad I made in Neufchâtel, which had a creamy dressing, this one has an incredibly refreshing and light dressing. Soak up any juices remaining at the bottom of your salad bowl with a piece of bread, or pour them over rice.

1. *To prepare the dressing,* crush the garlic. In a small bowl, mix with a pinch of salt.
2. Pour the oil over the garlic. Add the remaining ingredients and stir to combine.
3. Set aside to allow the flavours to develop. Check the seasonings, adding more lemon juice, salt and pepper to taste.
4. *To prepare the salad,* in a serving bowl, combine the salad ingredients. Pour the dressing over the salad and toss before serving.

VARIATIONS

Add 2 Tbsp finely chopped parsley and a handful of chopped green onions. Or use a combination of lettuce and ½ cup finely chopped cabbage and increase the amount of lemon juice to taste.

LEBANESE SALAD WITH TOASTED PITA, LEMON AND ZA'ATAR

FATTOULEH

While visiting my dearest old Palestinian friend, Aurora, I went with her to see her husband's family in Nazareth, where a number of Michael's eleven brothers and sisters, and dozens of nieces and nephews, lived. In every house we visited, we were served delicious dishes, and it would have been impolite to say no to them. Frankly, everything tasted so good, it was impossible to resist. Afterward, we went to the old market, where I bought about five pounds of spices. It was not that I could not find these spices in Canada, but these shops had an irresistible aroma and ambience, and the spices, sold in bulk, were fresher. The owners were so knowledgeable about spices that I felt I was given a crash course on their histories. I was like a kid in a candy store. After checking out each shop, we had worked up our appetites again, so went to our favourite Palestinian restaurant and ordered "the usual"—a collection of starters, including Lebanese salad (*fattouleh*).

1. *To prepare the dressing,* in a small bowl, pour the oil over the crushed garlic. Add the remaining ingredients. Set aside to allow the flavours to develop. Taste, and add more lemon juice if desired.
2. Meanwhile, *to prepare the salad,* in a serving bowl, combine the lettuce, mint, radishes, tomato, cucumber, parsley, pickles and onion. Pour the dressing over top but do not toss.
3. Toast the pita until it is dry and crunchy.
4. When ready to serve, toss the salad. Crumble the pita over top, then top with the feta cheese and eggs. Serve at once.

Serves 4

Salad

½ head Romaine lettuce, torn into bite-size pieces

10 mint leaves, chopped

2 radishes, chopped

1 tomato, finely chopped

½ English cucumber, finely chopped

½ cup parsley, finely chopped

½ cup chopped dill pickles or green or black olives

¼ cup finely chopped Spanish or other sweet onion, mixed with a pinch of salt

1 large pita

½ cup chopped feta cheese

2 hard-boiled eggs, quartered (optional)

Dressing

4 Tbsp olive oil

2 cloves garlic, crushed, with a pinch of salt

juice of 1 lemon

2 tsp za'atar (optional)

1 tsp sumac (optional)

1 tsp pepper

salt

MIDDLE EASTERN BREAKFAST

Suggested Ingredients

tomato

English cucumber

red, green and orange peppers

mushrooms

avocado

radishes

chopped sweet onions (mixed
with ½ tsp sumac, if desired)

pickles

olives

cottage cheese or labne
(page 16)

1 tsp za'atar per serving

1 to 2 tsp olive oil per serving

When I first moved to Europe, I worked for families who only ever had a couple of apples and oranges on the table. I was used to picking oranges in my backyard and eating five to ten of them a day! In the Middle East, you'll rarely see someone buy a single onion, tomato or cucumber. Going to a fruit and vegetable market in the Middle East is quite an experience. In one market I went to in Cairo, each stand sold a single kind of fruit or vegetable. One stand had just cucumbers; another had only watermelons. The vendors organized the produce in the shape of a pyramid, often with the salesperson sitting at the top, on the produce.

Cut vegetables with cottage cheese or labne are very filling, and a bowlful contains only a fraction of the calories of a muffin. In my house we often eat it as a snack or for breakfast. For years, my husband refused to eat vegetables with labne for breakfast, but gradually he converted to my kind of breakfast. Now he also adds za'atar and olive oil to the mix. I love to organize the vegetables by colour; it is quite beautiful. Each of us just turns the plate around and serves ourselves. We use toast or bread like a knife to push the vegetables onto the fork.

1. Cut the vegetables and pickles and place them on a large platter, along with the olives.
2. Serve with bowls of cottage cheese or labne, and za'atar and olive oil.

CRACKED WHEAT SALAD
TABBOULEH

Almost anyone who had eaten falafel or had any contact with Middle Eastern food has tasted tabbouleh. It is a great salad, but it does take time to chop the ingredients. My Palestinian friends can chop the parsley so fast, they're finished in the time it takes me to get the food processor out of the cupboard.

This salad keeps well in the refrigerator for a few days. Instead of pita, Lebanese and Palestinians often eat tabbouleh in the leaves of romaine lettuce, or wrapped in fresh cabbage leaves, which are very sweet when fresh. Sumac is available in Middle Eastern stores.

1. In a bowl, soak the cracked wheat in cold water for 30 to 60 minutes.
2. Meanwhile, in a salad bowl, combine the remaining salad ingredients.
3. Drain the cracked wheat. Using your hands, squeeze the excess water from the cracked wheat a little at a time before adding it to the salad.
4. In a small bowl, combine the dressing ingredients. Pour over the salad and toss to mix well. If you want more lemon, salt or pepper, do not hesitate to add it, starting with a small amount and adding more as desired.

VARIATION

To make a full meal of this salad, replace the cracked wheat with quinoa. At about 70%, the amount of protein in quinoa is very high. *To cook the quinoa:* Rinse 1 cup quinoa in a sieve under running water. In a medium pot over high heat, sauté an onion in 3 Tbsp olive oil. Add 2 cups chicken or vegetable broth, and salt and pepper to taste, and bring the mixture to a boil. Add the quinoa. Reduce the heat to medium-low and cook until all the liquid has evaporated, about 20 minutes. Let quinoa cool before adding to the other salad ingredients.

Serves 6

½ cup fine cracked wheat

2 bunches curly parsley (stems removed), finely chopped (or chop in a food processor for a few seconds)

3 tomatoes, very finely chopped

3 dill pickles, chopped, or ½ cup chopped black olives, plus more to taste

2 bunches green onions, finely chopped

½ small sweet onion, finely chopped

½ English cucumber, finely chopped

½ cup finely chopped mint leaves

Dressing

4 Tbsp olive oil

juice of 2 lemons

½ Tbsp sumac (optional)

1 tsp pepper

salt

TOMATO SALAD WITH PARSLEY, ONION AND LEMON

Serves 6

5 medium to large tomatoes, very finely chopped

½ cup parsley, finely chopped (or chop in a food processor for a few seconds)

1 bunch green onions, finely chopped

½ English cucumber, finely chopped

½ cup chopped sweet onion (mixed with a pinch of salt or sumac)

1 red or green pepper, chopped (optional)

3 radishes, chopped (optional)

½ cup fresh mint leaves, finely chopped

3 dill pickles, chopped, or ½ cup chopped green or black olives (optional)

Dressing

3 cloves garlic, crushed, with a pinch of salt

juice of 1 lemon

3 Tbsp olive oil

½ Tbsp sumac

1 tsp pepper

salt

In around 2006, I produced a documentary on the Israel-Palestinian conflict. As part of my research I travelled to the West Bank and Israel. One day, returning to Israel from Ramallah, in the West Bank, I found myself standing in a very long lineup at an Israeli checkpoint. It was quite painful to me to see elderly people humiliated by being shouted at and turned back, and children upset because they could not get to school, since the soldiers would not let them across. Babies were crying and pregnant women were growing weak in the heat. And the only way I can describe the soldiers is as scared-looking Rambos. The longer I stood in line, the angrier I got. But an older woman standing behind me punched me on the arm and quietly but firmly said, "Be quiet." As I turned around, the woman bent down and picked up a few fresh tomatoes from her bag and offered them to me. "Eat them," she said.

This salad is similar to the Cracked Wheat Salad, or tabbouleh (page 29), but without the cracked wheat and with less parsley, making it lighter. In Cairo, I saw men with buggies and donkeys in the market and on street corners selling breakfast. The breakfast consisted of *falloul* (beans) and salad. This is the salad they would serve. Iraqis rarely make salad with lettuce—for most Iraqis, "salad" means tomato salad.

1. In a salad bowl, combine all the salad ingredients.
2. Combine the dressing ingredients and pour over the salad, stirring to mix well. The amount of dressing is intentionally on the conservative side, but add more lemon, salt or pepper if desired.

CABBAGE SALAD WITH ZESTY MINT DRESSING

I was travelling with a friend in Chile in the early 1970s. Middle-class and wealthy housewives were on the streets, banging on their pots to protest against the economic policies President Allende was implementing. I was still semi-illiterate then and easily impressed by wealth. So when I saw the well-dressed women marching and banging the pots, they impressed me—or, more likely, they intimidated me.

It was only a few years later, after going to school, that I learned about the coup—General Pinochet's overthrowing, with the help of the CIA, of the democratically elected government of President Allende—and the subsequent brutalities and killings that thousands of Chileans endured under Pinochet's dictatorship. To think that I was there when this was happening but knew and understood so little about it.

Of all the salads I've tasted around the world, the one I ate in Chile is the most vivid in my memory, likely as much because of (looking back in retrospect) the period of history as because of the salad itself—though it certainly was tasty and distinctive. Like the salad I had in Chile, this cabbage salad is also very tasty and distinctive.

Unlike lettuce, cabbage does not wilt or become soggy after a day but retains its freshness. This salad tastes best if it stands for at least 1 hour to allow the flavours to develop.

1. In a large bowl, mix together the salad ingredients.
2. In a small bowl, gradually combine the dressing ingredients, starting with the garlic and half the lemon juice, oil, mint, pepper and salt and gradually adding more of each to taste, until the dressing has a lemony-mint flavour.
3. Pour the dressing over the salad, tossing lightly to mix. Let the salad sit for at least 1 hour before serving, tasting occasionally and adjusting the seasonings as desired, but keeping in mind that it takes time for the cabbage to absorb the dressing. It should have a touch of mint, garlic and lemon. If it doesn't, just add more seasonings, lemon juice, and olive oil a little at a time, stirring to mix.

VARIATION: CABBAGE SALAD WITH VINAIGRETTE

1. In a small bowl, combine the dressing ingredients and set aside.
2. In a deep serving bowl, combine the salad ingredients.
3. Pour in the dressing, tossing to mix.
4. Let salad stand for up to 1 hour so the dressing saturates the cabbage. Taste occasionally, adjusting seasonings as desired. If the dressing is too weak, add more olive oil, vinegar, salt and pepper, a little at a time.

Serves 6 to 8

1 small cabbage, very finely sliced

2 medium to large tomatoes, thinly sliced

½ English cucumber, thinly sliced

1 green or red pepper, thinly sliced

1 bunch green onions, chopped

Dressing

4 cloves garlic, crushed, with a pinch of salt

½ cup fresh lemon juice

4 Tbsp olive oil

4 Tbsp dried mint

2 tsp pepper

salt

Variation: Cabbage Salad with Vinaigrette

1 small cabbage, very thinly sliced

½ sweet onion, chopped

½ English cucumber, chopped

1 bunch green onions, chopped

1 cup chopped parsley

1 cup chopped dill pickles or green or black olives

Vinaigrette

5 Tbsp olive oil

¼ cup white vinegar

4 cloves garlic, crushed, with a pinch of salt

2 tsp pepper

salt

TUNA CABBAGE SALAD WITH WALNUTS AND NOODLES

Serves 6 to 8

1 pkg (10 oz/283 g) noodles of your choice, or more to taste

2 cans (6 oz/170 g each) tuna, drained, or 1 sautéed or broiled chicken breast, slivered

1 can (19 oz/540 mL) black beans or chickpeas, drained and rinsed, or 2 cups cooked dried beans (see page 156)

½ small cabbage, thinly sliced

2 large tomatoes, thinly sliced

1 red or green pepper, thinly sliced

½ English cucumber, thinly sliced

½ sweet onion, sliced

1 bunch parsley, chopped

1 cup chopped dill pickles or green or black olives

1 cup chopped roasted walnuts

1 cup frozen peas, steamed and drained (optional)

Dressing

5 to 6 cloves garlic, finely chopped, with a pinch of salt

4 Tbsp olive oil

4 Tbsp rice vinegar

¼ cup soy sauce

¼ cup fresh lemon juice

1 Tbsp Dijon mustard (optional)

2 tsp pepper

In the early 1990s during my travels across Canada researching a series on first-generation Canadian immigrants, I interviewed an elderly Jewish couple who lived in Toronto, survivors of the Second World War. Upon my arrival at their home, they asked if I was hungry. I politely answered no, but the wife brought me cabbage salad, served with tuna and a fresh piece of bread. She and her husband insisted that I eat before starting the interview.

During the war they had both been active in the resistance movement in Poland. While they were on the run, the woman had given birth to her baby. They described an incident in which they were hiding in the back of a horse-drawn buggy, covered with hay, when the buggy was stopped by German soldiers. The wife held the baby tight against her breast, almost choking him, praying he would not cry. They survived six years on the run before going to a refugee camp and eventually immigrating to Canada. In Canada, they earned their living as garment workers and raised two children. For many years they all lived over a bakery in a one-bedroom apartment. I asked the couple what their happiest moments were. They talked about the birth of their two children and watching them grow and become successful doctors. Maybe this salad is not exactly what I was served, but its aroma reminds me so much of that beautiful encounter.

NOTE: You can use a package or two of Chinese chicken noodle soup for the boiled noodles if you like.

1. In a bowl, combine the dressing ingredients and set aside.
2. Cook the noodles according to the package directions; drain.
3. In a large salad bowl, combine the salad ingredients, including the drained noodles.
4. Add the dressing and toss to mix. Do not hesitate to add more lemon juice or soy sauce for extra zest.

EGGPLANT AND CORIANDER SALAD
WITH LEMON DRESSING

Serves 4 to 6

At one point, I produced a series of radio documentaries on the war in Chiapas between the Mexican central government and the landless indigenous population of southern Mexico. One night I went to the restaurant of my hotel in San Cristobal with a couple of other journalists. I had just come from a day of interviewing at the cathedral, where hundreds of locals, along with journalists and human rights activists, had gathered. It was the only time during my travels that I had put every piece of identification and all my money in a pouch around my waist. I was planning to leave town the next morning, and because of the government's war with the Zapatistas, there were roadblocks and checkpoints where I would be required to present my identification to army officers.

We ordered whatever the kitchen had left in the way of food, which turned out to be eggplant salad, served with tortilla. We sat at the table for a couple of hours, unwinding and talking about the day's events. When finally I went to pay my bill, I discovered that my pouch was gone. I panicked. I had no ID—not a single piece of paper that said "My name is Souad Sharabani"—and I had no money. In a panic, I phoned the owner of the hotel. He advised me to go to the military headquarters right away.

Because Chiapas was a war zone, the army personnel were on edge, and the hotel owner was kind enough to accompany me. At headquarters, the soldiers carried machine guns, and there was a continuous stream of people being brought in handcuffed. In English mixed with broken Spanish, I explained to an officer what had happened, but I got the feeling he didn't believe me. After all, with my black hair and olive skin, I could be mistaken for a Mexican. I was at the army's mercy, and if it didn't want to give me the paper I needed to leave, I would have been stuck there for a long time. The officer made me wait for hours, then finally gave me the piece of paper that allowed me to leave the province and, later, the country.

When I think of my time in Chiapas, I am reminded of that night in the restaurant, and of the eggplant salad I had. This recipe is my own version and is magnificent. It keeps well in the refrigerator for at least 3 days. You can serve it as a side dish or add chickpeas to turn it into a meal, with bread on the side. Enjoy!

1. Place the eggplant cubes on a baking sheet lined with parchment paper; they don't need to lie flat.
2. Sprinkle with salt, pepper and olive oil and bake in a 400°F oven for 20 to 25 minutes, until light brown and cooked through. Remove from the oven and set aside to cool.
3. Meanwhile, in a large salad bowl, combine all remaining salad ingredients. Add the cooled eggplant.
4. In a separate bowl, combine the dressing ingredients; pour over the salad and toss to mix.

1 eggplant, cut lengthwise, then cubed

salt and pepper

olive oil, for sprinkling

3 dill pickles, sliced, or ½ cup green or black olives, chopped, plus more to taste

3 mushrooms, chopped (optional)

3 radishes, chopped (optional)

2 medium tomatoes, chopped

1 red, green or yellow pepper, finely chopped

½ English cucumber, chopped

½ small Spanish onion, chopped, sprinkled with a pinch each of salt and sumac

1 bunch green onions, chopped

1 bunch fresh coriander or parsley, chopped

1 can (19 oz/540 mL) chickpeas, drained and rinsed, or 2 cups cooked dried chickpeas (see page 156)

Dressing

4 cloves garlic, crushed, with a pinch of salt

5 Tbsp olive oil

juice of 2 lemons

2 tsp pepper

salt

1 Tbsp sumac (optional)

PALESTINIAN CUMIN CARROT SALAD

Serves 6 to 8

2 lb carrots, sliced

1 large sweet onion, finely
    chopped

1 bunch parsley, chopped

Dressing

8 cloves garlic, crushed, with a
    pinch of salt

¾ cup fresh lemon juice

5 Tbsp olive oil

2½ Tbsp cumin

1 Tbsp pepper

salt

In 2006, I spent some time in the West Bank producing a documentary on Palestinian-Israeli writers and poets talking and writing about the conflict. No one can express the feelings, the fears, the hatred, the hopes and aspirations of a people better than their own poets and writers; they are the heartbeat of their people and of their nations. That is why I produced dozens of documentaries examining writers and poets from around the world.

In Ramallah, I interviewed a Palestinian poet named Zakaria Mohammed. It was an ordeal just to get to him: there were roadblocks, fences and checkpoints. What really struck me was the severe deterioration in the standard of living since my last visit, in the mid-1980s. There was complete economic dysfunction, and the infra-structure had been destroyed. During my previous visit, I had seen an abundance of fruit and vegetables and other foods, but not this time. Instead, I saw poverty and despair everywhere I turned.

Mr. Zakaria was waiting for me at a restaurant, where we ordered appetizers. One of the dishes we ate was marinated carrots. We talked at length about current politics, hope and despair. His sadness and despair were obvious as he talked about his people. I asked whether his politics and his poetry were one and the same given the circumstances he lived under. He answered, "Poetry is a very fragile vase. Poetry needs to be treated like God; you need to worship him alone, and if you worship another God with him, you might destroy him. On the other hand, the violence day by day is directly in my poetry. You can smell the flame and the smoke in my poetry."

Mr. Zakaria read me one of his poems:

The Horse
The boy watched the black horse with the white star set in his forehead,
The black horse watched nothing.
He lifted one hoof from the ground.
The meadow was lush under the scorching sun.
The horse's star blazed under his forelock.
The horse wore no bridle, he had no bit in his mouth,
Still he chomped and chomped, whirring his head while hot blood
    spilled from his lips.
The boy was amazed. "Why is the black horse chomping?" he asked.
    "What does he chomp on?"
The black horse is chomping on a bit of memories forged from cold steel
    to be chomped on and chomped on till death ...

◈　◈　◈

1. Steam the carrots for 25 minutes or until tender. Drain the carrots and transfer to a serving bowl.
2. Meanwhile, in a small bowl, combine the dressing ingredients, starting with only 1 Tbsp of the cumin and adding more to taste.
3. Add the onion and parsley to the hot carrots. Immediately add the dressing, tossing to coat. Season with more lemon juice, salt, pepper and cumin to taste.

FENNEL SALAD WITH ORANGE VINAIGRETTE

2 fennel bulbs, trimmed and
thinly sliced

1 small sweet onion, thinly sliced

1 cup black or green olives,
sliced

1 bunch parsley or coriander,
chopped

3 medium apples or pears
(peeled or unpeeled), cored
and thinly sliced

Dressing

¼ cup white vinegar

¼ cup olive oil

juice of 2 oranges

salt and pepper

Fennel is not a common vegetable in the Middle East. I rarely cooked it until I began shopping at an Italian grocery store in Toronto where recipes were generously shared between shoppers and employees. Fennel has a distinct, anise-like sweet flavour. I was told to cook it with onion and garlic or to put it in a salad. One day I had a couple of fennel bulbs that I wanted to use up, so I decided to make a salad with it. It was delicious.

Let the fennel marinate in the dressing for at least 1 hour before serving, to allow the flavours to develop. The salad keeps well in the refrigerator for 2 to 3 days.

1. In a large serving bowl, combine the fennel, onion, olives, parsley and apples.
2. In a separate bowl, combine the dressing ingredients. Pour over the salad and toss to mix well.
3. Let stand for 1 hour, then adjust seasonings to taste.

MANGO SALAD

I ate mangoes frequently during my travels in Latin America and India, and since they're readily available year-round in North America, I now buy them every week. I eat them just as pieces of fruit, or make a smoothie, cold soup, or salad with them. One day, I was eating my mango salad, looking over a proposal I had written, in preparation for a conference call with funders. The proposal was for a series of radio documentaries following a group of teachers who were going to India to do volunteer work and learn first-hand about the complex socio-economic conditions of the poor people of India.

A few days before the conference call, we had got a new puppy at home. My son and my husband had set up a crate for the dog in my son's room, across the hall from my office. They promised me that as long as the puppy could see and hear me, he would not bark. My son went to school and my husband went to the office and the dog stayed with me, barking non-stop. As the time for the conference call neared, I grew so nervous, I could not even finish my mango salad.

The phone rang and I answered it, and we started to discuss the project. But I could hardly hear anything above the dog barking. After a few minutes, I politely said, "I am sorry, can you excuse me for a minute?" I pressed the hold button, then yelled as loud as one can possibly yell, "Shut up or I will kill you!"

Of course, the puppy did not quiet down, but I had no choice—I released the hold button—or so I thought—to continue the conversation. "As I was saying ..." I stopped when I heard giggles. Then one of the callers asked, "Who are you planning to kill—your husband or your kids?"

This salad makes a great side dish. It is full of flavour.

◇　◇　◇

1. In a bowl, combine all the ingredients. Stir to mix well and enjoy.

Serves 4

5 ripe mangoes, peeled, pitted, and cut into small pieces

juice of 3 limes

3 Tbsp chopped coriander

3 Tbsp finely chopped sweet onion

Tea garden, Nepal, 1998

For Iraqis, main-course dishes are usually stews, so soup is rarely served with the meal. On some occasions, though, like cold winter days, we might make thick chicken soup with rice and cardamom for breakfast. But in my travels around the world, experiencing different cuisines, I have eaten and later prepared the most exquisite soups: South African–style squash soup; Darjeeling-style chicken soup; gazpacho, a Spanish cold vegetable soup. I usually serve soup with a hearty piece of fresh bread, as a meal in itself.

SOUPS

Spinach Lentil Soup with Garlic, Mint and Lemon

BEET SOUP
BORSCHT

Serves 6 to 8

1 large onion, chopped

4 Tbsp olive oil

2 beef shank bones (approx 2 lb), well rinsed

water, enough to cover the meat

1 can (28 oz/796 mL) whole or crushed tomatoes

5 beets, peeled and cubed

2 potatoes, quartered

2 medium carrots, sliced

½ small cabbage, sliced

6 bay leaves

2 cubes chicken bouillon

½ cup fresh lemon juice

2 Tbsp sugar (optional)

1 Tbsp pepper

salt

Years ago I worked on a series of documentaries dealing with stories of first-generation Canadian immigrants. I travelled from coast to coast collecting dozens upon dozens of stories of people from all walks of life and with family tracing back to all parts of the world. It was in rural Alberta where I met with people from the oldest German farming community in the country. Some had arrived in Canada before the First World War. The man I was scheduled to meet with came to the bus stop in his pickup truck to take me to his home. Although he must have been in his nineties, he drove pretty aggressively.

When we got to his house, he took me directly to the kitchen, where his wife had prepared borscht and homemade dark rye bread for us. After eating and drinking I set my tape machine, with its ninety-minute tape, and the microphone on the table. As soon as I asked the man the first question, he started talking—and did not stop. He reminded me of the Energizer bunny. My head started to feel heavy and I just could not keep my eyes open. Regrettably, I fell asleep while he was talking and woke up only when I hit my head on the microphone, toppling it over. I was startled and apologetic, but the man seemed to have not even noticed; he was still happily talking. The tape machine had already stopped, but I did bother to tell him or change the tape; I just let him continue talking for a while longer.

Whenever I go to a Hungarian or a Jewish restaurant, I unfailingly order borscht as an entrée. It is very light and very tasty. Serve topped with a spoonful of sour cream if you like.

1. In a deep pot, sauté the onion in the oil over low heat.
2. Add the shank bones and enough water to generously cover the bones. Increase the heat to medium-high, bring to a boil, and cook for 15 to 20 minutes, skimming off any fat and foam from the surface. When the broth is almost clear, add the remaining ingredients and more water if needed to cover the vegetables.
3. Bring the broth to a boil, reduce the heat and cook on a low simmer for at least 1½ to 2 hours, until the vegetables are tender and the meat has fallen off the bones. Halfway through cooking, taste and adjust spices, lemon juice or water. The soup should taste sweet and sour. Before serving, remove and discard the bones.

CHILLED VEGETABLE SOUP
GAZPACHO

This is one of my favourite cold soups during the summer, and it keeps well in the refrigerator for a few days. When I travelled through Spain, there was no better lunch to have than a bowl of gazpacho. In Spain, the vegetables are chopped into small pieces, instead of being puréed. There are very few things that taste fantastic that we can eat as much as we wish without putting on weight. Gazpacho is one of them.

1. Combine the tomato juice, lemon juice, olive oil, garlic, pepper and salt in a large, deep bowl.
2. In a food processor, coarsely chop the vegetables and herbs (chop a bit at a time).
3. Add the chopped vegetables to the tomato juice mixture. Stir to mix well, adding more lemon juice, salt or pepper to taste.
4. Serve the soup at room temperature or chilled.

Serves 6 to 8

1 can (48 oz/1.36 L) tomato juice

½ cup fresh lemon juice

4 Tbsp olive oil

4 cloves garlic

2 tsp pepper or 1 jalapeño pepper, chopped (remove seeds for less heat)

salt

6 tomatoes

1 English cucumber

1 small sweet onion

2 sweet peppers (green, red, yellow or orange, or combination)

2 bunches green onion

1 bunch coriander

½ cup fresh mint leaves

CHILLED MANGO SOUP

Serves 8 to 10

10 mangoes, peeled, pitted and sliced

3 cups plain yogurt (2% to 3.5% MF)

2 cups chicken or vegetable broth

2 cups milk (1% to 3% MF)

½ cup chopped mint leaves

3 Tbsp maple syrup (optional)

2 tsp nutmeg

1½ tsp ground ginger

peel of 1 lemon, grated

The mango soup I ate in Baratnagar, India, when I was there doing a documentary on the lives of workers in tea gardens, will always have a special meaning for me.

I never knew how beautiful, lush and green the tea gardens are. Tea bushes themselves are not that tall, but in Baratnagar they were surrounded by palm trees to create shade. The tea leaves—simple, small green leaves—were picked by the workers at what seemed like the speed of light. At the end of the day, the dozens upon dozens of men and women lined up at the processing factory to weigh the leaves they had picked that day—they are paid by weight. The women were stunningly beautiful, wearing the most magnificent colourful saris. I spent some time with them in the fields and in their homes.

On my first day there, as the sun was setting and I walked with them to their village, they seemed very anxious. I asked why. They explained that because it was monsoon season, elephants came down the mountains in herds of up to two hundred and travelled through the tea gardens as they migrated to their next destination. If an elephant loses its herd, it becomes very aggressive, often smashing everything in sight. As a result, the locals built their bamboo huts high enough off the ground so that the elephants could not reach them, but it was dangerous to be out in the fields after sunset.

After an hour of walking we reached the home of a local tea workers' organizer, a proud and strong woman. The home, more like a room, was very modest but filled with warmth. As we sat down we were served mango soup. As we sat talking, eating and drinking, I heard an extremely loud rumbling noise in the distance. Before I could ask what it was, my companions smiled and said, "Those are the elephants in the tea gardens."

◈ ◈ ◈

1. Purée ingredients in a food processor, in batches if necessary.
2. Refrigerate for 30 minutes to allow flavours to meld. Adjust ingredients to taste—you may want to add more spices, mint, milk, even mango.

SWISS CHARD AND BEAN SOUP
SOPA CON CARNE

I've eaten Swiss chard in many countries, but the most memorable time was in Malawi, at St. Mary's Orphanage for children with HIV/AIDS, outside the capital. I was producing a documentary in a six-part radio series on southern Africa. What struck me about the orphanage was that it was not a depressing, miserable place— far from it. It was run by a group of nuns from India and Latin America and by streams of volunteer doctors, nurses, teachers and students from around the world, all of whom gave love and energy to the place.

Some of the children had been at the orphanage since they were newborns. When they turned sixteen, they would be given a little money to help them settle in their home village and build themselves a hut. At the orphanage, the children lived in groups of five or six in small, well-furnished homes, each with a designated "mother." The food was cooked collectively in a big kitchen, but the children ate in their homes. The orphanage had a farm where the staff, volunteers and older children grew vegetables and raised animals.

My most moving experience there was at the Sunday service, which lasted for half a day. People from the orphanage and the neighbouring villages came for it. All the orphans were dressed in clean, brightly coloured clothes. The chanting and dancing were so beautiful and infectious, you couldn't help but join in. Yet, only next door in the hospital, mothers and children lay sick with malaria, malnutrition and AIDS.

Each evening, after a day of being surrounded by the wonderful children and selfless staff, I appreciated and loved every bit of the humble meal of Swiss chard and maize. This chard and bean soup gives me the same feeling of comfort as that meal at the orphanage did.

1. Heat the oil in a deep pot over low heat. Sauté the onions and garlic until light golden.
2. Add the shank bone and water to cover. Bring to a boil, skimming off any foam from the surface.
3. Add the remaining ingredients, and more water if necessary to cover the ingredients. Bring to a boil, reduce the heat to simmer, stir, and cook until the ingredients are tender and the meat has fallen off the bone, about 2 to 2½ hours.
4. Taste, and season with salt and pepper as desired. Remove and discard the bone before serving.

Serves 8 to 10

4 Tbsp oil

2 onions, chopped

1 head garlic, chopped

1 beef shank bone

water, enough to cover ingredients

4 to 6 oz chorizo, sliced (optional)

2 cans (19 oz/540 mL each) white kidney beans, rinsed and drained, or 3 cups cooked dried white kidney beans (see page 156)

2 potatoes, quartered

2 tomatoes, chopped (optional)

2 carrots, chopped

1 bunch Swiss chard or kale, chopped

½ small cabbage, chopped

6 bay leaves

3 cubes chicken bouillon

1 bunch parsley, chopped

1 Tbsp pepper or 1 jalapeño pepper, chopped (remove seeds for less heat)

salt

St. Mary's Orphanage, Malawi, 2001

SPINACH LENTIL SOUP WITH GARLIC, MINT AND LEMON

Serves 6

1 cup dried green or brown lentils or 1½ cans (19 oz/ 540 mL each) green or brown lentils, drained and rinsed

1 large onion, chopped

1 head garlic, chopped

4 Tbsp oil

4 Tbsp dried mint

1 tsp pepper

salt

3 pkgs (10 oz/284 g each) fresh spinach

½ cup long-grain white rice, soaked in cold water for at least ½ hour, then drained, or 1 cup orzo

3 cups boiling water

juice of 2 lemons

2 cubes vegetable or chicken bouillon

This Lebanese dish is a meal in itself if served with bread. It's a great winter dish and such a healthy dish, not to mention very fast to cook. In Zambia, I tried a vegetable that I can only describe as being something between spinach and Swiss chard. It grew on the Kasisi organic farm, in Lusaka, the capital of Zambia.

Crossing Zambia by land, what struck me was the destruction of the countryside. Fires burned in the fields and on the hills, and my throat and eyes stung from the smoke in the air. At one point I was on the road for about eighteen hours, travelling to a town called Katondwe. The heat, fire and smoke were unbearably close. I looked around and wondered, what is there for people to eat? I felt the hopelessness and helplessness that was setting in.

The Zambian student of agriculture accompanying me explained that Zambian agriculture used to be far more self-sufficient. But the agricultural base had been ruined by continued droughts and the government's policy of eliminating agricultural subsidies to farmers. As a result, most Zambians could not afford to buy fertilizer or seeds to plant on their farms. Everyone I talked to reiterated the same message loud and clear: malnutrition and famine, malaria and illiteracy in Africa can be prevented only if poverty is eliminated and a sustainable economy built.

In the midst of all this devastation, there are pockets of successful endeavours aimed at building a local, sustainable agricultural base. I visited one such project, the Kasisi Agricultural Training Centre. Kasisi has alleviated poverty and brought dignity and prosperity to thousands of Zambians. Brother Paul, a Canadian Jesuit who studied agriculture at the University of Guelph, in Ontario, moved to Zambia over thirty years ago and started the Kasisi project. Now, the work and the training are done by Zambians for Zambians.

Kasisi is a fifteen-minute drive from Lusaka. When I arrived in Kasisi, I saw a very unfamiliar sight in that part of Africa: rows and rows of trees and cultivated land. Farmers and their families from all over Zambia come to Kasisi for training that lasts from six months to two years. They learn about organic cultivation, irrigation techniques, toolmaking and establishing cooperative farming. They are also able to save money from selling in the city the produce they grow at Kasisi. With that money, they buy the tools and seeds they need to farm their own land. Upon returning to their villages, they share their newly acquired knowledge with other farmers. And the knowledge keeps on spreading to thousands upon thousands of farmers.

We arrived at Brother Paul's modest accommodation, where he prepared a lunch for us. One of the dishes he made was with the spinach/Swiss chard–type vegetable. He was very proud to tell me, "Everything we are eating grows on this land."

◇   ◇   ◇

Victoria Falls, Zambia, 2001

1. Cook the lentils (if using dried) in a pot of salted water over medium heat for about 25 minutes or until they are very tender. Drain and set aside.

2. Rinse and dry the pot and return it to low heat. Sauté the onion and garlic in the oil until light golden.

3. Add the mint, pepper and salt. Increase the heat to medium-low, then gradually add the spinach, one package at a time, covering the pot and letting the spinach wilt before adding the next batch.

4. Add the cooked lentils, rice, water, lemon juice and bouillon cubes. Stir to mix well.

5. Simmer for at least 20 to 30 minutes, until the rice is cooked. Taste and make sure the soup has a subtle lemon and mint flavour—it should not be too lemony. If you need more mint or lemon, add a little at a time. If the soup is too thick, add more water, ½ cup at a time. As soon as the rice is cooked, remove from the heat and serve.

CREAMY CHARD AND POTATO SOUP
SOPA VERDE

Serves 6

3 Tbsp oil

1 large onion, chopped

1 head garlic, chopped

4 potatoes, quartered

1 bunch Swiss chard or kale, chopped (stalks included)

2 cubes vegetable or chicken bouillon

2 Tbsp dried dill (optional)

2 tsp pepper

salt

4 to 6 oz chorizo, sliced (optional)

water, enough to cover ingredients

In Toronto, my husband and I lived in a Portuguese neighbourhood; two neighbours in particular I will always remember: Emanuel and Maria. With Maria, nothing was ever out of place. I think she made the beds in the middle of the night if one of her kids or her husband made the mistake of getting up to go to the washroom. Maria liked to give me tips on how to keep my house cleaner. She also loved to share her great cooking with me. She would bring over either *sopa con carne* or *sopa verde* almost once a week, more often when I was pregnant, because she felt I needed to be fed some good hearty Portuguese food.

This is a very simple but very tasty Portuguese soup, one that can be made in almost no time. The sausage, which is optional, has a distinct, strong flavour.

1. Heat the oil in a deep pot over medium heat. Sauté the onion and garlic until light golden.
2. Add the vegetables, bouillon cubes, seasonings, sausage (if using) and enough water to cover the ingredients.
3. Bring to a boil, then reduce the heat; simmer for 25 to 35 minutes, until vegetables are tender. Adjust seasonings to taste.
4. Purée the soup with a hand blender until creamy.

SOUTH AFRICAN-STYLE SQUASH SOUP

When I think of squash, I'm reminded of the soup I had in South Africa. It was to die for, and I ate it almost everywhere I went in Cape Town. From Cape Town I went to Stellenbosch, an hour or so away by train. With its rolling hills and lush greenery, it was beautiful and serene. Not far from there, I visited a co-op organic farm called SPIR that had started after the end of apartheid. For generations, the farm workers had provided cheap labour. Dirt poor, they had no proper housing, schooling for their children or prospects for the future. When apartheid ended, these workers took over the farm. With some government assistance and professional expertise, they cultivated as co-owners the land that they and their families had worked on for generations. These farmers are now running successful organic farms. With the profits they are able to expand the business and also build modest homes. They have great dreams for their children. It is a true success story.

Not far from the organic farm, I stopped at a quaint restaurant. Once again, I ordered squash soup. The soup and bread I was served were out of this world. I have tried to recreate that squash soup strictly by memory of its scent, and this version tastes close to it. I usually use Hubbard squash, but feel free to use any kind you like. This soup will keep in the refrigerator for several days.

1. Cut the squash into quarters and scoop out and discard the seeds.
2. Place the squash on a baking sheet lined with parchment paper, sprinkle with cinnamon and olive oil and cook in a 375°F oven for 20 minutes or until the squash are partially cooked and easy to peel. Remove from the oven and peel once cool to the touch.
3. Meanwhile, in a large, deep soup pot, melt 2 Tbsp of the butter; sauté the onion, garlic and ginger (if using) until golden.
4. Add another 2 Tbsp of the butter, the apple, vegetables, bouillon cubes, water-and-milk mixture, maple syrup and spices.
5. Bring to a boil; add the peeled squash and stir. Reduce the heat and simmer for 35 to 45 minutes, until the vegetables are very soft.
6. Turn off the heat. Add the milk, coriander and the remaining 2 Tbsp butter; purée the soup with a hand blender. Adjust seasonings and milk to taste—the soup should be creamy and slightly spicy.

Serves 6 to 8

2 squash of your choice

cinnamon, for sprinkling

olive oil, for sprinkling

6 Tbsp butter or margarine

1 large onion, chopped

1 head garlic, chopped

1 Tbsp chopped ginger (optional)

3 apples or pears, cored and sliced

2 carrots, peeled and sliced

2 potatoes, peeled and sliced

1 sweet potato, peeled and sliced

2 cubes chicken or vegetable bouillon

6 cups combination of water and milk (or enough to cover vegetables)

3 Tbsp maple syrup

2 cups milk

1 bunch coriander, chopped

Spices

2 Tbsp curry powder

2 Tbsp cinnamon

2 Tbsp allspice (optional)

2 Tbsp nutmeg

1 Tbsp ground cloves

2 tsp pepper

salt

TOMATO SOUP WITH ZUCCHINI AND FRESH BASIL

Serves 6 to 8

5 Tbsp oil or butter

1 large onion, chopped

1 head garlic, chopped

1 can or tube (5½ oz/156 mL) Italian tomato paste

1 can (28 oz/796 mL) crushed tomatoes

1 Tbsp anchovies (optional)

2 cubes vegetable or chicken bouillon

6 large tomatoes, chopped

2 large zucchini, chopped

2 large potatoes, quartered

1 bunch basil, chopped

2 Tbsp dried oregano

equal parts milk and water, enough to cover ingredients

1½ tsp pepper

salt

2 cups milk

I love tomato soup, though for years I thought it too complicated to make. But I played with the texture, aroma and flavour and came up with this simple and tasty soup. For me, it symbolizes everything I felt in Monte Blanco, Peru—warmth, comfort and being very close to the earth.

After my endeavour to climb a mountain in Peru failed miserably, I spent some time living with a peasant family in the foothills of Monte Blanco. The family was extremely poor, existing on a subsistence income from the little they grew on their plot of land. I felt that there was something so beautiful and pure about the people and the village that I asked if I could stay behind with them instead of returning to Arequipa with the other mountain climbers. They embraced me as a member of their family.

Every morning I joined the family and their donkey in the fields. Each person from the age of three and older had a task to do. In the evenings when we returned home at sunset, the women prepared something to eat, which always involved some form of corn. Afterward, as we lay in our own corners of the dark room, the children and the adults would ask me to tell them stories about my childhood, where I came from, and about Europe and North America, all in my broken Spanish.

One morning on our way to the fields, the mother turned to me and said, "I am about to have my baby. Go with my children to the fields." She did not want me or anyone else to help her. I saw her bending down behind the trees. I have no idea how she cut the umbilical cord. After lunch she joined us in the field with the newborn.

For me, this tomato soup symbolizes the purity of those people's lives and the bond between earth and man, which was one of mutual respect.

◇   ◇   ◇

1. Heat 2 Tbsp of the oil in a deep pot over medium heat. Sauté the onion and garlic until light golden.
2. Add the tomato paste, crushed tomatoes, anchovies (if using), bouillon cubes, vegetables, herbs, milk-and-water mixture, pepper and salt. Stir to mix well.
3. Bring the mixture to a boil. Reduce the heat and simmer for 35 to 45 minutes, until the vegetables are very soft.
4. Remove from the heat and gradually add the milk and the remaining 3 Tbsp oil while blending with a hand blender. Taste and adjust ingredients, adding more milk, herbs, salt or pepper, even more oil, as desired.

CHICKEN RICE SOUP WITH CARDAMOM

Many Iraqis make this thick soup in the wintertime, sometimes eating it for breakfast. I loved waking up to the smell of it slow-cooking on the stove. Since we often fed this soup to people who were sick, whenever I eat it I cannot help but think of my time volunteering in Calcutta at Kalighat, the home for the dying homeless run by Mother Teresa's volunteers.

One person I assisted was a tiny woman, not much more than a skeleton, who was lying in bed almost motionless. I asked one of the nuns if she would like me to feed this woman. She handed me a cup of broth and said, "This patient does not have much time to live. She is not eating or drinking." I started to feed her, but she barely responded. I rubbed her arm and her forehead, all the while chatting, telling her about myself and my children. She took the food very slowly. But when I stepped away for a minute, I saw her hand reach for mine and her eyes open for a few moments. I rushed back, started to cry and held her hand even tighter. I put my face against hers and stayed that way until she let go of my hand.

1. Drain the soaked rice and set aside.
2. In a deep pot, heat the oil over low heat. Sauté the onion until light golden.
3. Add the tomatoes and parsley; sauté for 2 to 3 minutes. Add the chicken, bouillon cubes, tomato paste and spices.
4. Pour in water to cover the chicken. Increase the heat to medium-high and bring the mixture to a boil.
5. Reduce the heat and simmer slowly for at least 1 hour, until the chicken meat is falling apart. Taste the soup occasionally to make sure it has enough spice—the flavouring should be fairly strong, since the rice will mellow the spice once it is added. Remove the chicken and set aside.
6. Add the rice to the soup, and more water and spices, if needed, a little at a time.
7. When the chicken has cooled to the touch, remove and discard the skin and bones. Cut the meat into slivers and return to the pot, stirring to mix. The soup should be quite thick.

Serves 6 to 8

2 cups long-grain white rice, soaked in cold water for 1 hour

4 Tbsp oil

1 large onion, chopped

2 tomatoes, finely chopped

1 cup parsley, finely chopped

¼ medium whole chicken, cut into pieces (skin on)

2 cubes chicken bouillon

4 Tbsp tomato paste

1½ Tbsp allspice

1 Tbsp pepper

1 tsp turmeric

seeds from 12 cardamom pods, crushed (optional)

salt

water, enough to generously cover chicken

Tea garden, Darjeeling, 1998

DARJEELING-STYLE CHICKEN SOUP

Before travelling there, I knew nothing about Darjeeling other than in relation to tea. Darjeeling is in the foothills of the eastern Himalayan mountain range, and I was there working on a series of documentaries on Canadian Jesuits in the region.

After driving for six hours along winding roads from Siliguri, West Bengal, we reached the breathtaking mountains. Women dressed in beautiful, colourful saris could be seen in the distance picking tea leaves in the foothills. The climate changed from 110°C with 100 percent humidity to dry, chilly 10°C temperatures. The eighty-kilometre drive through the narrow roads was treacherous, taking nearly six hours. Parts of the road had been washed away by mudslides, leaving huge gaps covered only with plywood and rocks. This was even less reassuring after I saw rows of flowers on the roadside left in memory of the casualties of car accidents there.

Even though Darjeeling is part of India, it is linguistically and culturally Nepalese. Homes are built on the mountainsides, and I could feel the steep 60-degree incline as I walked up and down the narrow unpaved streets and steps. I was in Darjeeling during monsoon season, when it doesn't just rain but pours, and with very little break. Mudslides due to deforestation were a common sight, and many houses were left clinging to the mountain, the land dropped out from beneath them. Thousands of people have lost their homes this way.

During my time there, I often stopped at one of the tiny local teahouses or restaurants to warm up. The first thing I asked for was hot tea with a touch of lemon juice, ginger and sugar. And then I would ask for chicken soup, which was a very simple one but equally delicious.

1. *To prepare the soup,* in a large soup pot, heat the oil over medium heat. Sauté the onions, garlic and ginger until golden.

2. Add the remaining soup ingredients. Bring to a boil, then reduce the heat and simmer for 1 to 1½ hours. Taste occasionally, adjusting seasonings as desired. When the bones are about to fall apart, remove from the pot and discard.

3. *To prepare the chicken mixture,* in a frying pan or wok, heat the oil. Sauté the slivered chicken breasts with 1 Tbsp of the soy sauce until the meat is cooked through.

4. Add the remaining 3 Tbsp soy sauce, the lime juice and sesame oil, along with the bean sprouts, spinach and green onions. Sauté for 2 to 3 minutes.

5. Add the chicken mixture to the soup pot, stirring to mix. Taste and adjust ingredients, adding more soy sauce, rice vinegar, lime juice, pepper or sesame oil as desired.

6. *To prepare the noodles,* bring a pot of lightly salted water to a boil. Remove from the heat and add the rice noodles; let stand until soft, 5 to 10 minutes.

7. Drain the noodles and spoon into individual soup bowls. Ladle the soup over top and serve.

Serves 6

1 pkg (16 oz/454 g) rice noodles of your choice

Soup

2 Tbsp oil

2 large onions, chopped

1 head garlic, chopped

3 Tbsp grated ginger

3 to 4 chicken backs

6 cups water (or enough to generously cover ingredients)

2 cups green peas

1½ cups grated carrot

2 cubes chicken bouillon

4 Tbsp rice vinegar

salt and pepper

Chicken Mixture

2 Tbsp oil

2 chicken breasts, slivered

4 Tbsp soy sauce

3 Tbsp lime juice

2 Tbsp sesame oil

3 cups bean sprouts

1 bunch spinach, chopped

1 bunch green onions, chopped

With the exception of a few recipes, when I cook vegetable or legume dishes I make them as a main course. In my travel and work around the world, I had the honour of living with people from different cultural and ethnic backgrounds. More often than not, I lived among the most disenfranchised people in those societies, from those in a tuberculosis and leprosy colony in India to poor peasants in remote areas of Chiapas, Mexico. The food I ate with them was predominantly vegetable and legume based. These dishes are affordable to make and full of flavour.

VEGETABLES AND LEGUMES

Potato Latkes with Spinach and Fresh Herbs

IRAQI BOILED BEETS AND TURNIPS
SHELRAM

Serves 6

3 small to medium beets, scrubbed and quartered

1 small turnip, scrubbed and cut into big chunks

2 Tbsp sugar

1 Tbsp salt

scant handful loose black tea leaves

water, enough to cover the vegetables

My father told me that vendors in Baghdad sell *shelram* in the markets or at roadside stands. At home, we usually left this dish to simmer for many hours, sometimes all day, and people would just help themselves from the pot.

I remember, when I was growing up in Israel, my dad coming home for lunch in the wintertime; the first thing he did was put on his *abaia*—a long, warm cape made of camel skin. Wearing the *abaia,* my dad looked imposing. He would then sit on the wooden bench by the front door eating boiled beets with turnips. The rest of us—me, my brothers, my mother and often a neighbour or a family friend—sat either on the floor or on tiny footstools around the Hibachi, warming our hands. Nearby, on a little gas stove, the big pot of boiled beets and turnips had been bubbling away since breakfast time. This dish fills the house with a very strong smell, but it has a very nice sweet flavour. Serve as a side dish; there's no need for a dressing.

1. In a large soup pot over high heat, bring all the ingredients to a boil.
2. Reduce the heat to low; simmer for at least 2½ hours, until the vegetables are very tender.
3. Remove the beets and turnips from the liquid to serve.

FRIED EGGPLANT

My husband's grandmother, originally from Romania, referred to eggplants as black tomatoes. Part of Iraqis' staple diet, cooked eggplants have a rich, creamy texture. A week didn't pass that we didn't eat eggplants when I was growing up. Every Saturday morning we ate hard-boiled eggs, salad, pickles, pita and eggplants—sliced, salted and fried. To this day, my siblings eat this meal for Saturday morning breakfast. Fried or baked eggplant is also often served as a side dish.

Serves 4

1 medium eggplant

salt, for sweating eggplant

pepper, paprika, dried rosemary and/or basil, for sprinkling (optional)

½ cup olive oil (approx), for frying

1. Slice the eggplant into rounds about 1-inch thick. Sprinkle with salt and other seasonings (if using) and let stand for 1 hour in a strainer.
2. In a shallow frying pan, heat the oil until very hot. Reduce the heat to medium and add the eggplant to the pan, in batches if necessary. Turn once to brown both sides. Transfer to a plate lined with paper towel to absorb any extra oil.

VARIATION: BAKED EGGPLANT

Instead of frying, bake the eggplant on a greased baking sheet or one lined with parchment paper. If there is not enough room to spread the eggplant in a single layer, sprinkle the first layer with olive oil and seasonings (if using), then place a layer on top, sprinkling it as well with oil and seasonings (if using). Bake at 400°F for 25 to 30 minutes, checking after 25 minutes, until the skin is browned and the flesh is very tender. If you like the eggplant crispy, reduce the temperature to 325°F and bake for another 10 to 15 minutes.

BAKED EGGPLANT WITH CURRIED LEGUMES AND TOMATOES

Serves 6

2 medium eggplants, sliced into 1-inch rounds

salt and pepper

4 Tbsp olive oil, plus more as needed

8 cloves garlic, chopped

2 large tomatoes, chopped

1 large onion, sliced

1 red pepper, thinly sliced

1 bunch parsley, finely chopped

1½ cans (19 oz/540 mL each) legumes of your choice (such as chickpeas, kidney beans, black beans), drained and rinsed, or 3 cups cooked dried legumes of your choice (see page 156)

Spices

2 Tbsp curry powder

1 Tbsp paprika

1½ Tbsp cumin

1 Tbsp pepper

salt

Sauce

1 can (28 oz/796 mL) crushed tomatoes

1 cup boiling water

¼ cup rice vinegar

2 cubes vegetable or chicken bouillon

2 Tbsp ketchup (optional)

1 Tbsp sugar

When I was growing up, I was picked on by both the teachers and the children at my school. The only friend I had was a girl named Batia, who was in the same situation as me. Another girl from school, who was also my neighbour, regularly made fun of me and my friend and threw things at us.

One day Batia and I were standing outside, minding our own business, and the girl, as usual, started to call us names, telling us we were stupid and dirty. Batia and I had had enough of her. Instead of crying and running inside, we pulled her into an empty shed and stuffed hot peppers in her mouth, something my great-uncle had told us he did to stray cats on his farm when he wanted to get rid of them. The girl ran away so fast, screaming, and never bothered us again.

More than forty years later, my brother, who is a criminal lawyer, visited a maximum-security prison to meet with a client. One of the prison guards, a big, robust woman, looked at my brother's identification papers and then stared at him.

"Is there a problem, officer?" my brother asked.

"Do you have a sister called Shoshana?" she asked, referring to me by my Hebrew name.

He proudly said yes and asked her how she knew me.

The guard's face turned red as she recounted what I had done to her more than four decades earlier, warning my brother that if she ever saw me she would punch the living daylights out of me.

Unlike the sensation of hot peppers, this dish fills your mouth with great flavours and aroma.

1. On a greased baking sheet or one lined with parchment paper, arrange the eggplant slices and sprinkle with salt, pepper and olive oil. Bake in a 400°F oven for 20 minutes (they do not have to be fully cooked). Set aside.

2. Spread 4 Tbsp olive oil on the bottom of a deep casserole dish. Add the garlic, tomatoes, onion, red pepper, parsley and legumes; stir to mix.

3. In a small bowl, combine the spices. Add half of the spice mixture to the vegetables, stirring to coat well. Add the eggplant.

4. Add the sauce ingredients to the reserved spices, stirring to blend. Pour the sauce over the vegetables, stirring with a fork so that the sauce coats the vegetables evenly. Drizzle a little olive oil over top.

5. Bake in a 400°F oven for 1¼ to 1½ hours, stirring every 30 minutes or so and adjusting the spices to taste. The liquid should taste slightly sweet, with a touch of curry flavour.

6. When the liquid has almost evaporated and the vegetables and legumes are very soft, reduce the heat to 325°F and bake for another 1 hour. Then turn off the oven but leave the dish inside until you are ready to eat. Serve over rice.

GREEN BEANS WITH TOMATOES, GARLIC AND ONION

PASOULIYI

This dish is popular in the Middle East. Do not use frozen beans, as they will become mushy. I had a similar dish in Damak, Nepal, where I was working in the late 1990s on a radio documentary about the refugees from Bhutan who settled in camps around Damak, on the border with India. Two groups of people have settled there: migrant workers from southern India who worked the land as day labourers, and refugees from Bhutan. According to testimonies of Bhutanese refugees, the royal family of Bhutan had executed policies of ethnic cleansing, resulting in the expulsion of thousands of people. Some estimate that one of every six Bhutanese is a refugee, most living in the refugee camps in southeastern Nepal.

I spent some time with a group of volunteers at one of the camps and recorded a documentary about the state of the camps. I was impressed by how well organized the refugees were. They had well-run schools and social and medical services to which the local Jesuits contributed a great deal. I met a Bhutanese surgeon who chose to stay and help his people in the camp rather than move out, even though he would be better compensated elsewhere. He and every other man, woman and child in those camps was eager to return to Bhutan. You only had to look at the children's drawings or read their short stories to understand the impact of fear, uncertainty and longing. When it was time to say goodbye, I felt very sad leaving them, as though I were leaving them behind prison bars.

Among our group of volunteers were a couple of Jesuit priests, an Irish nurse and a doctor. One night we were all invited to the priests' residence, where we prepared something to eat. Since the experience of the day had been so overwhelming and the conditions so unfamiliar, eating together was comforting; I was happy to be surrounded by people who spoke a language I spoke and who shared common experiences. We prepared dinner—the electricity going off and on all the while—and talked politics. One of the dishes we made was green beans, though it was definitely spicier than this one. Serve this as a side dish. Leftovers keep well in the refrigerator for several days.

Serves 6

4 Tbsp olive oil

1 large onion, chopped

1 head garlic, chopped

2 large ripe tomatoes, finely chopped

1 red pepper, sliced

1½ lb green beans, trimmed

1 bunch parsley, chopped (optional)

4 Tbsp water

1 cube vegetable or chicken bouillon

salt and pepper

1. Heat the oil in a pan over low heat; sauté the onion and garlic until light golden.
2. Add the tomatoes and red pepper; cook for 5 minutes, covered.
3. Add the beans along with the remaining ingredients; stir to mix well. Simmer for 45 to 60 minutes, to allow the beans to cook well with the vegetable juices. If the dish is too dry, add 2 to 3 Tbsp water.

STEWED CABBAGE WITH RED BEANS AND TOMATOES

Serves 6 to 8

4 Tbsp oil

1 large onion, sliced

1 head garlic, chopped

2 tomatoes, chopped

1 small cabbage, thinly sliced

1 cup boiling water

¼ cup rice vinegar (optional)

1 can (28 oz/796 mL) crushed tomatoes

1 can (19 oz/540 mL) red and/or white kidney beans, drained and rinsed, or 2 cups cooked dried red and/or white kidney beans (see page 156)

2 carrots, sliced (optional)

1 bunch parsley, chopped

2 cubes chicken or vegetable bouillon

2 Tbsp coriander seeds

2 tsp pepper or sliver of jalapeño pepper

salt

Student trip to Zambia, 2001

The most memorable cabbage dishes I have eaten were in Zambia and Malawi, where as a radio producer I documented a group of teenage Canadian students who were travelling and volunteering mostly at orphanages—playing with the children and comforting those who were ill, assisting the teachers in the classrooms and helping in the fields.

Road travel was treacherous. One day, we witnessed a horrendous bus accident. We all jumped out of our vans to help, but it was too late. There were dozens of dead and wounded, and the nearest hospital was three hundred kilometres away. It was a frightening experience for all of us, and although we knew we could not help the seriously wounded, we tried to comfort them. The nurse and the dentist among us administered first aid, while the rest of us hoped and prayed that ambulances would arrive soon. I was so proud of the students: each and every one of them was eager to help regardless of any danger to themselves.

We eventually continued on our way, driving in silence, still in shock, and reaching our destination, a priests' residence, a few hours later. Altogether, we had been on the road for seventeen hours. The building we were staying in was extremely modest; there were no beds—we just put our sleeping bags down on the floor. Just before dark, a few of us went to a nearby market for food. We wanted to cook something filling but tasty. By the time we returned, the sky was almost pitch black. In the tiny kitchen, which had a small counter, a small two-burner gas stove, two big pots and a tiny sink and table, we tried to cook quickly, since the electricity was unreliable. It went out soon after we began, but we continued with flashlights strapped to our foreheads. We could not wash anything with tap water, nor could we cook with the water. We had to be careful to sterilize the water first so we could wash the vegetables and also leave enough clean water for cooking. We grew excited about eating a warm meal, and started getting creative.

After two hours of hard work, we had made a dinner of cabbage, beans and rice. The only spices we had to use were salt and hot pepper. But there were no leftovers that night. I do not know whether it was because we were so hungry or because it was such a fine meal. I had such a beautiful, warm feeling seeing our group, sitting every which way, sharing our humble meal. Especially after witnessing a deadly accident, I appreciated life and being alive.

I've altered the cabbage dish we cooked in Zambia that night just a little, since I have more choices for spices and vegetables now. Serve with or without rice as a main dish.

◇   ◇   ◇

1. Heat the oil in a deep pot over low heat. Sauté the onion and garlic until light golden.
2. Add the tomatoes and cook for 2 to 3 minutes.
3. Add the cabbage, 2 cups at a time, and sauté for 2 to 3 minutes, until wilted. After all the cabbage has been added, cook for about 5 to 7 minutes.
4. Add the remaining ingredients.
5. Increase the heat to medium-high, stirring often to prevent burning. Once the mixture has reached a boil, reduce the heat and simmer for at least 35 to 40 minutes, stirring occasionally, until the vegetables are tender. Taste halfway through cooking, adding water, salt and pepper if needed.

FAVA BEANS WITH MINT AND LEMON
HAMEES

Fava beans are very popular across the Middle East. There are regular green fava beans, which are cooked in stews; small green ones added to rice, especially in Iranian cooking; and split fava beans, used for falafel. The large brown variety is either roasted or boiled. Anywhere you go in Egypt, especially in the markets, you'll find food stalls selling salads, pita and boiled fava beans, or *hamees*. Egyptians often eat fava beans for breakfast. Many Iraqis snack on them the way North Americans do with peanuts. Whenever my dad played backgammon, he'd have a bowl of hot boiled fava beans flavoured with lemon juice and mint beside him to nibble on.

Fava beans are easy to cook and, once cooked, will keep in the refrigerator for 3 to 4 days. For this recipe you can use dried, fresh or canned fava beans. (Dried beans need to be prepared in advance, so plan ahead.) If using dried, don't eat the skin—it will slide off easily in your mouth. Fresh beans are often available in Italian food stores when in season.

Serves 6

1 cup fresh large brown fava beans or cooked dried brown fava beans or 1 can (19 oz/540 mL) brown fava beans (see Step 1)

1½ Tbsp dried mint

juice of 1 lemon

salt and pepper

1. If using *fresh* fava beans, remove and discard the shells, then boil the beans for 20 minutes in salted water. If using *dried* fava beans, soak in water for 24 hours, then boil until soft, about 2 hours. If using *canned,* rinse and drain.
2. In a serving bowl, toss the prepared beans with the mint, lemon juice, and salt and pepper. Eat cold or hot.

SWEET CARROT CASSEROLE WITH ORANGE AND RAISINS

TZIMMES

Serves 6

1½ cups vegetable broth

2 Tbsp cornstarch

2 lb carrots, grated

1 small sweet onion, chopped

4 apples, peeled, cored and
    grated

½ cup raisins

1 cup orange juice

½ cup fresh lemon juice

4 Tbsp olive oil or butter

2 Tbsp sugar (optional)

1 Tbsp pepper

salt

This is a typical eastern European Jewish side dish, and a very sweet one. It is often made during the High Holidays. For me, this dish brings back memories of the generosity of strangers.

Soon after immigrating to Canada, I got a job selling tchotchkes from house to house, and on industrial and construction sites. Promised a cut of the profits and opportunities to travel and see the country, I and other uneducated, new immigrant women took our employers—two men—at face value and drove with them in a van from Montreal to various small towns in Ontario. We stayed in rundown motels just off the highway, four to five girls to a room. We worked from the early hours of the morning until nighttime but were lucky if we made $35 a week. Out of that we had to pay for our food. After a while I started to complain, telling the men that they were cheating us of our money and should pay us more. They didn't take kindly to that.

One evening back at the motel, one of the men asked me to pack my bag. He told me that I was no longer welcome, that I was a bad influence on the others. He gave me a few dollars and dropped me off on the highway between Hamilton and Burlington, Ontario. My first reaction of rage turned to panic when I realized that I didn't even have enough money for a motel that night. I found a phone booth and looked in the telephone directory for a Jewish name, phoning the first one I saw: Cohen. A man answered and I told him I was a Jewish woman who had lived in Israel and that right then I was stranded by the highway. He gave me the rabbi's number. I phoned the rabbi and told him my story. He made a few calls and found an elderly Jewish couple who were willing to come and pick me up.

I am not a religious person, but when I saw the couple approach the phone booth, it was like seeing angels. They took me in, gave me a hot meal, kept me for a few days and then gave me enough money to pay for a bus ticket to Montreal and for a month's rent. I wish I remembered their names. I do remember distinctly the meal I was served that first night in their home. It must have been around the Jewish High Holidays because they served chicken and a sweet noodle dish and what I now know as *tzimmes*. Eating it, I felt like I had gone to heaven and back.

◇　◇　◇

1. In a bowl, whisk together the broth and cornstarch. In a deep bowl, stir together the remaining ingredients, then transfer to a deep baking dish. Pour in the cornstarch mixture. Adjust seasonings to desired sweetness. Bake in a 400°F oven for 40 to 45 minutes, until the vegetables are extremely soft.

This version can be served either as a side dish or as a main course.

Serves 6

1. Place the shank bones, water, onion, salt and pepper in a Dutch oven and bring to a boil. Reduce the heat and simmer for about 30 minutes, skimming off any foam from the surface.
2. Meanwhile, in a small bowl, combine the dressing ingredients.
3. Add the remaining casserole ingredients and the dressing to the shank bone mixture, stirring to mix well.
4. Bring to a boil, reduce the heat and simmer for 2 hours (or bake in a 400°F oven for 1½ hours), until the meat falls off the bone and the carrots and potatoes are tender. Halfway through cooking, stir well and taste to make sure the dish is sweet, with a touch of cinnamon and nutmeg. Add more orange juice and spices as desired. Add more water if the dish is too dry.

Casserole

2 beef shank bones, rinsed and patted dry

4 cups water (or enough to cover bones)

1 large onion, chopped

salt and pepper

2 lb carrots, sliced

2 sweet potatoes, peeled and cut into rounds

2 cubes chicken bouillon

½ cup raisins (optional)

Dressing

1 cup frozen orange juice concentrate, thawed

juice of ½ lemon

2 Tbsp brown sugar (optional)

2 Tbsp lemon peel

1 Tbsp cinnamon

1 Tbsp nutmeg

1 tsp paprika

MARINATED CARROTS

Serves 6 to 8

2 lb carrots, scraped and
   cut in half crosswise and
   lengthwise

1 to 2 tsp prepared mustard

Marinade

¼ cup dry white wine

¼ cup white wine vinegar

¼ cup olive oil

¼ cup water

6 cloves garlic, minced, with a
   pinch of salt

5 bay leaves

3 sprigs thyme (or 1 tsp dried)

1 tsp salt

1 tsp sugar

When I was a child, my dad forced me to drink a glass of carrot juice every day after a friend told him that carrots were good for weak eyes. Each day we walked to the corner kiosk, where the vendor squeezed a glass of fresh carrot juice for me. I would be forced to drink it while the other kids had ice cream, or at least a glass of fruit juice. I felt like I was being tortured. Despite this childhood experience, there are some carrot dishes and salads that I love very much. This recipe belongs to my colleague Edna. This dish is easy to make and keeps for 1 to 2 weeks in the refrigerator.

1. Combine the marinade ingredients in a large saucepan and bring to a boil.
2. Add the carrots and boil, uncovered, until the carrots are just tender when pierced with a knife. (Cooking time will vary depending on the size and age of the carrots.) Using a slotted spoon, transfer the cooked carrots to a shallow serving dish.
3. Add the mustard to the warm marinade, stirring to blend. Pour over the carrots and allow carrots to cool.
4. Serve at room temperature or chilled.

HERBED CARROTS, POTATOES AND SQUASH

I first had a dish like this one in Siliguri, West Bengal. I was producing a radio documentary on Jesu Ashram Hospital, a hospital for leprosy and TB patients. The hospital was founded and overseen by the late Brother Bob Mittelholtz, a Canadian Jesuit from Guelph, Ontario, and by the late Sister Ivana, a Croatian nun who moved to India with Mother Teresa. When I met Sister Ivana at Jesu Ashram, she was close to ninety years old. One day as I was interviewing Brother Bob, a tiny woman entered his office. Although short and slightly bent over, she had a powerful presence. I barely noticed her age or physical appearance so taken was I with her dynamic energy. Sister Ivana, however, was fuming and didn't even notice that a stranger (me) was present. She was upset about the final score in a soccer match between Croatia and France. France had won.

Sister Ivana was a multitasker. In control of the hospital's finances and day-to-day operation, she also assisted with the planting and harvesting of the fields, and helped the poor and the destitute who lived outside the hospital gates. Being the nurse, Sister Ivana also visited each and every patient daily. One patient was complaining of pain and fever. Sister Ivana gave her a hug and said, "Don't worry, we will look after you." She then turned to me and said, "This woman must be reacting to her medication. She is feeling sad … everyone needs some warmth, sympathy and a touch." She sat on the bed, holding the woman's hands and chatting with her. As I watched from a distance, Sister Ivana noticed how nervous I was—it was my first visit to a leprosy colony. She pulled me toward her and said, "These patients are not infectious, and you should not be afraid to get close to them. Hold this lady's hands; she would like that very much. And don't pretend, do it from your heart."

Seeing how moved I was, Sister Ivana smiled and said, "Come on, let's go to the kitchen. I am starving." She paused for a moment, then said, "There is one more thing I have to do. Come with me to the fields." As we walked, she told me that usually she rode her scooter there. After about twenty minutes we reached the fields where the residents of Jesu Ashram grow their vegetables, rice and legumes. Several people were there, planting rice. As we drew closer, I could tell that Sister Ivana did not approve. She pushed up her dress and walked into the muddy field to show the workers the proper way to plant the rice.

Sister Ivana, with a few helpers, prepared the meals for the patients. When we got to the kitchen, she tasted the prepared dishes. "Ha!" she said. "Once again there are not enough spices in the food." She turned to me and said, "Just because we are serving sick and poor people does not mean we should serve them tasteless food!"

One of the dishes she served was vegetable casserole—a fabulous dish. I have replicated it here, but with more vegetables and spices. Serve over white rice.

Serves 6

3 carrots, peeled and sliced

1 acorn squash, peeled and cubed

1 sweet potato, peeled and sliced into rounds

2 potatoes, cubed (unpeeled)

2 stalks celery, chopped

2 cubes vegetable bouillon

1 large onion, chopped

1 head garlic, chopped

3 cups water

3 Tbsp oil

2 Tbsp each dried oregano and thyme

1 Tbsp each pepper and dried basil

1 tsp nutmeg

salt

1. Place all the ingredients in a deep casserole dish and stir to mix well.
2. Bake in a 425°F oven for about 1 hour, until the vegetables are very tender. Stir after 30 minutes and adjust seasonings to taste. If it is too dry, add more water, a little at a time.

CURRIED CAULIFLOWER AND SWEET POTATO CASSEROLE

Serves 6

4 Tbsp olive oil

1 large onion, chopped

1 head garlic, chopped

2 Tbsp chopped fresh ginger or ground ginger

2 tomatoes, chopped

1 bunch parsley or coriander, chopped

1 pkg (10 oz/284 g) fresh spinach

1 can (19 oz/540 mL) chickpeas, drained and rinsed, or 2 cups cooked dried chickpeas (see page 156)

3 cups water

2 medium potatoes, cubed (unpeeled)

2 carrots, sliced (unpeeled)

2 zucchini, sliced (unpeeled)

1 small cauliflower, cut into small pieces

1 sweet potato, cubed (unpeeled)

1 cup frozen peas

4 Tbsp rice vinegar

juice of 3 limes

2 cubes chicken or vegetable bouillon

2 Tbsp curry powder

1½ Tbsp coriander seeds

1 Tbsp pepper or 1 jalapeño pepper, chopped (remove seeds for less heat)

salt

During my visit to the Jesu Ashram Hospital in Siliguri, West Bengal, I met lepers known as the stone breakers. They lived near the hospital in a town called Matigara, earning a poor living breaking stone and selling the gravel to gravel companies. It was one of the few jobs that lepers could do because of the social abhorrence of their disease. Stone is hard to come by in the foothills of the Himalayas, but each year monsoons swept stone down the Balasun River near where they lived on hospital property by the riverbank.

Mike, the chief surgeon at Jesu Ashram, had, like some of the stone breakers, been a leprosy patient there. I was completely taken by his remarkable story. A humble, illiterate man, Mike was found on a train platform, very sick, homeless and hungry. He was brought to the hospital by Brother Bob. After several operations and a long recuperation, like the other ex-leprosy patients, he stayed to live on the hospital property. These former patients are the rejects of society and are never reintegrated back into the community.

Mike began helping out wherever he was needed, and he was particularly keen to assist in the operating room. Sister Ivana, who managed Jesu Ashram and who was also its sole nurse, first let him wash instruments, then pass instruments during operations. When the doctor, a French surgeon, saw Mike so eager to learn, he took him under his wing and trained him until he felt confident to let Mike operate himself, first with supervision, and later without supervision. A few years later, the French surgeon left and Mike replaced him as the sole surgeon at the hospital.

After watching Mike in the operating room, I followed him on his rounds. What struck me about this man was not just the incredible story of his transformation from a poor, illiterate, sick man into a surgeon without formal education but how this transformation had not affected his gentle, kind character.

The day I met Mike at Jesu Ashram, we had cauliflower casserole for lunch. Serve this dish over rice, or with chapattis, as Sister Ivana did.

1. Heat the oil in a deep frying pan or pot over low heat. Sauté the onion, garlic and ginger for a few minutes, until light golden.

2. Add the tomatoes and parsley; cook for 3 to 4 minutes. Increase the heat and, stirring, gradually add the remaining vegetables, then all the remaining ingredients.

3. Bring the mixture to a boil, reduce the heat and simmer for 45 to 60 minutes, until the vegetables are tender and juicy. Stir occasionally and adjust spices to taste. Add more water, a little at a time, as needed.

SPICED BAKED CAULIFLOWER

Baking cauliflower may be an unusual way to prepare it, but the result is very tasty. I had this dish in Kenya when I was invited for lunch at an acquaintance's home in a suburb of Nairobi. I had just spent some time in a shantytown outside Nairobi, where people lived in what were practically cardboard boxes. It was a culture shock to go from there to a huge estate with gardeners, cooks, doormen and butlers. And in the magnificent dining room a butler served us the most delicious Indian food. One of the dishes was baked cauliflower.

Black garam masala is available at Indian food stores.

1. In a large bowl, combine the dressing ingredients.
2. Add the cauliflower, stirring to mix well. Turn out onto a greased baking sheet or one lined with parchment paper.
3. Cook for 25 to 30 minutes in a 425°F oven until the cauliflower is tender-crisp.

Serves 6

1 large cauliflower,
    cut into florets

Dressing
3 Tbsp olive oil
3 Tbsp sesame seeds
1 Tbsp coriander seeds
1 Tbsp black garam masala
    (optional)
1 tsp pepper
salt

FRESH HERB FALAFEL

Makes 20 to 30 falafel balls

1 cup dried chickpeas
1 cup dried small split fava beans
1 large onion, halved
½ head garlic
1 bunch green onions
½ bunch coriander
½ bunch parsley
1 Tbsp cumin
1 tsp pepper
salt
4 Tbsp all-purpose flour
2 tsp baking powder
vegetable oil, for deep-frying

The best falafel I have ever had was in Egypt. Unlike Palestinian falafel, which is made predominantly with chickpeas, falafel in Egypt is light and full of greens and fava beans. In Cairo's Khan el-Khalili Souk, falafel comes in a paper cone with pickles. I love it and almost every day went to the *souk* to sit in a café, drink strong, bitter Arabic coffee, eat falafel and watch the passers-by. You can imagine that the ambience of a market that has been there for over a thousand years is fantastic. And you can find almost anything in the tiny stores lining the narrow, dark streets—from spices to prepared food to jewellery. And everywhere there are people, walking, talking and hollering—it was a real commotion. I felt very much at home there.

To make falafel a full meal, serve warm in pita, preferably the paper-thin kind, along with Cabbage Salad with Zesty Mint Dressing (page 31), pickles, tahini and hot sauce. Sometimes I add sliced cucumber, tomatoes, sweet onion and sprigs of parsley. Don't mix the vegetables like a salad; instead, serve in individual bowls for people to help themselves. Sometime I also include slices of baked or fried eggplant (page 55).

The falafel mixture can be prepared in advance, then portioned to make several meals. Freeze unused portions in resealable bags. (Thaw in the refrigerator for at least 24 hours; do not microwave.) The chickpeas and fava beans need to soak first for at least 8 hours, so plan ahead. Do not use canned or cooked fava beans for this recipe, as they will disintegrate in the oil. The cooking oil can be poured into a jar once it has cooled, then kept in the freezer, to reuse another two times.

1. Rinse and pick over the chickpeas and fava beans, then soak in a generous amount of cold water (they will expand) for at least 8 hours, changing the water several times. Drain and rinse, then spread on a kitchen towel to let them dry a little.

2. Using a food processor, combine the chickpeas, beans, onion, garlic, green onions, coriander, parsley, cumin, pepper and salt, a little at a time. Process to a smooth paste.

3. Portion out half of the mixture to freeze for later, if you wish. Stir the flour and baking powder into the remaining portion (double the amounts if you are going to fry all of the mixture). Let stand for at least 30 minutes.

4. In a deep pot suitable for deep-frying, heat enough oil to cover the falafel. When the oil is very hot, very gently drop in the falafel mixture, a tablespoonful at a time. Do not overcrowd—cook in batches if necessary. Cook for a few minutes, until slightly brown and crisp. Remove with a slotted spoon and drain on paper towel.

5. Serve immediately, or keep warm in the oven until ready to serve.

CHILI-CUMIN LENTIL CURRY

At home when I was growing up, lentils were often used in rice dishes and stews, but rarely were they served on their own as a meal. After travelling to Mexico, India and Nepal, I better understood the role of the legume as a staple part of the daily diet. The Nepalese eat a lentil dish for breakfast, the flavours and vegetables in it changing with the seasons. The Nepalese do not use a lot of hot spices, relying on more subtle flavouring.

In the small Nepalese town of Pokhara—where, on a clear day, you can see Mount Everest in the distance—I documented the work of the Jesuits among the poor and the destitute. The owner of the bed-and-breakfast where I stayed was kind enough to invite me and a couple of other guests for supper at his home. We sat on the rooftop while his wife cooked right there in front of us. We were conversing simultaneously in three languages: English, Nepali and Punjabi. Through body language and sheer effort, I managed to be part of the conversation.

The husband recounted what had happened to him and his wife on their wedding night. After the ceremony, he and his wife returned to his parents' home, where they would live for many years. But his parents' home was a small one, with only one bedroom shared by many brothers and sisters. That night, in the dark, he could not find his wife among the bodies lying next to him. At one point he stretched out his arm hoping he was touching his new bride, but it was his sister-in-law, who yelled "Don't touch me!"

His dear wife, who was cooking as he spoke, commented, "I never told you how relieved I was not to consummate our wedding that night …"

Later that night, the wife served us supper on a simple foil platter with four or five compartments, each filled with a differently flavoured lentil dish; in the centre was white rice. Some of us ate with our fingers; others used spoons or a piece of chapatti. The dinner was so very tasty.

1. If using dried lentils, pick over for small stones, then rinse and generously cover with salted water. Bring to a boil, reduce the heat to medium-low and cook until very soft, about 25 minutes. Drain.
2. Meanwhile, warm the oil in a pot over low heat. Sauté the onion, garlic, ginger and jalapeño pepper until light golden.
3. Add the tomatoes and parsley. Cook over low heat for 3 to 4 minutes.
4. Add the remaining vegetables, spices, lentils and water, stirring to mix.
5. Cover the pot and bring the mixture to a boil. Reduce the heat and simmer for 45 minutes or until the vegetables are very tender. Halfway through cooking, adjust seasonings to taste; the dish should have a slight curry-cumin flavour. Add more water if needed, though the mixture should not be too watery.

Serves 6

2 cans (19 oz/540 mL each) green lentils or 1½ cups dried green lentils

3 Tbsp oil

1 large onion, thinly sliced

10 cloves to 1 head garlic, chopped

1 Tbsp chopped ginger

1 jalapeño pepper, chopped (remove seeds for less heat)

2 medium tomatoes, thinly sliced

1 cup chopped parsley

2 potatoes, cut into small pieces

2 carrots, sliced

½ small cauliflower, cut into small pieces

2 Tbsp cumin

1½ Tbsp curry powder

1 Tbsp coriander seeds

2 cubes vegetable or chicken bouillon

salt

4 cups water (or enough to cover ingredients)

LENTIL RICE PUDDING

Serves 6

1½ cups dried green lentils

4 Tbsp oil

1 large onion, chopped

1 head garlic, chopped

2 cups water

½ cup long-grain white rice, soaked in cold water for 1 hour, then drained

1 cube vegetable or chicken bouillon

1 tsp pepper

salt

When my son was a baby, Juju, his Lebanese nanny, made this dish for him at least once a week. Watching Beno and Juju eat lunch together warmed my heart. He never sat in his high chair but always on her lap, and she would talk and sing to him while they ate. As Beno grew older, I often heard him talking to Juju in beautiful Arabic with a Lebanese dialect. When he graduated from the baby food she made for him, she prepared any meal he wanted. No wonder it was tough for Beno to adjust first to nursery school and then to elementary school—life was just great with Juju!

This dish just melts in your mouth. It is healthy and a perfect dish for babies because it is puréed. Lebanese eat this dish with yogurt and bread on the side. It has the texture of thick pudding.

1. Pick over the lentils for small stones, then rinse. Bring to a boil in a large pot with lots of lightly salted water. Reduce the heat to low and cook for at least 25 minutes, until lentils are tender. Drain and set aside in the strainer.

2. In a large pot over low heat, heat the oil. Sauté the onion and garlic until light golden.

3. Increase the heat to medium and add the remaining ingredients, including the lentils. Stir and bring to a boil.

4. Reduce the heat and simmer for at least 20 to 25 minutes, until the rice is cooked. Season with more salt and pepper to taste.

5. Purée the ingredients with a hand blender or in a food processor, then simmer for another 5 to 10 minutes.

6. Transfer to a large serving bowl or individual bowls. Let cool before serving.

CURRIED LEGUMES WITH TOMATOES

Father Horrigan from the Toronto Area Interfaith Council asked me if I would be interested in doing a documentary about Kids4Peace Camp, a program in which Canadian children of Christian, Muslim and Jewish backgrounds are brought together with Palestinian and Israeli children to spend two weeks in a camp in northern Ontario. I was very excited to take part in such endeavours—anything that would help bring peace to the region. A Pakistani couple drove me to the camp, about three hours away. Along the way, we stopped to eat a most beautiful lunch they had packed, which included a lentil and split pea dish.

At the camp I was pleasantly shocked by what I saw. A counsellor told me that when the children first arrived, they were nervous and did not talk much because of their preconceived notions about each other. But after being together for a while, the myths and half-baked truths that they had brought with them were stripped away, layer by layer.

When I talked to the children, they repeatedly said, "I thought we were different, but now I know we are all the same. We all have the same feelings." A bond of deep love, respect and trust developed among these children. They laughed and played together, each one speaking their own language—Hebrew, English or Arabic—and each wearing their own style of dress—some girls wore veils, others shorts.

This lentil and split pea dish is similar to the one I ate on the way to the camp. Serve as a side dish or as the main course with a salad. The legumes need to be soaked for at least 8 hours, so plan ahead.

1. Pick over the lentils and split peas, removing any small stones. Soak in cold water overnight, changing the water a few times. Rinse and drain.
2. Heat the oil in a pot over low heat; sauté the onion, garlic, jalapeño pepper (if using) and ginger until light golden.
3. Add the tomatoes, cover and cook for 3 minutes.
4. Add the lentils, split peas, tomato paste, milk-and-water mixture, bouillon cubes, spices and 2 Tbsp of the butter.
5. Bring to a boil, reduce the heat and simmer for 2 to 2½ hours, partially covered, until the lentils and split peas are very soft. Stir often to prevent burning on the bottom. Halfway through cooking, adjust the spices or liquid as desired, adding a little at a time. You should be able to taste the gentle flavours of the spices.
6. When the lentils and split peas are cooked, add the 2 cups of milk, the remaining 3 Tbsp butter and the coriander. Serve as it is or purée with a hand blender to a creamy consistency.

Serves 6 to 8

¾ cup dried red lentils

¾ cup dried split peas (combination of green and yellow)

3 Tbsp oil

1 large onion, chopped

1 head garlic, chopped

1 jalapeño pepper, chopped (remove seeds for less heat) (optional)

2 Tbsp chopped ginger

2 large ripe tomatoes, chopped

1 can (5½ oz/156 mL) tomato paste

equal parts milk and water, enough to generously cover ingredients

3 cubes vegetable or chicken bouillon

5 Tbsp butter

2 cups milk

1 bunch coriander, chopped

Spices

2 Tbsp cumin

2 Tbsp curry powder

1 Tbsp freshly grated nutmeg

1 Tbsp dried coriander

2 tsp turmeric

2 tsp ground cloves

salt

HERBED OKRA WITH GINGER

Serves 4 to 6

4 Tbsp oil

2 Tbsp chopped ginger

1 large onion, sliced

1 head garlic, sliced

2 large tomatoes, thinly sliced

1 green or red pepper, chopped

2 stalks celery, sliced

1 bunch parsley or coriander, chopped

1 Tbsp coriander seeds

1 Tbsp cumin

1 Tbsp curry powder

2 tsp pepper or chopped jalapeño pepper (remove seeds for less heat)

1 tsp turmeric

salt

2 pkgs (10 oz/300 g each) frozen okra or 2 lb fresh okra, trimmed

Sauce

1 to 2 cubes chicken or vegetable bouillon

1 can (14 oz/398 mL) tomato sauce

juice of 1 lemon (optional)

2 cups water (or enough to just cover ingredients)

In Calcutta I worked on a documentary about the red light district, visiting one of the city's poorest districts, where people live in what can only be described as tiny boxes, often containing just a bed and a chair. The distance between the homes is the same—only as wide as two people standing side by side. You can practically touch your neighbour's home when you spread out your arms. I asked people with families how they all fit in one room. Very casually they told me that they sleep in shifts.

The cooking is done in the tiny alleyways between the homes, which are covered with plastic coverings during the rainy season. I watched the women as they sautéed onion, garlic, herbs and okra on tiny gas burners. It looked and smelled good, and I am sure it tasted good as well. Here is my version. I serve this dish over white or red rice.

1. In a deep pot, warm the oil over low heat. Add the ginger, onion and garlic; sauté until light golden.
2. Add the tomatoes, pepper, celery and the herbs and spices; sauté for 5 to 7 minutes.
3. Increase the heat to medium and add the okra.
4. Meanwhile, in a separate bowl, combine the sauce ingredients. Pour over the okra mixture, stirring gently.
5. Increase the heat slightly and bring the mixture to a boil, stirring gently to prevent burning on the bottom. Once the mixture comes to a boil, reduce the heat and simmer for about 45 minutes, until the okra is tender. Add more lemon juice or seasonings to taste, a little at a time. The okra should have a subtle lemon taste, with a distinct flavour of herbs.

BOILED ONIONS WITH CHEESE
JEBAN BEL BASEL

In the Middle East it is common to eat vegetables for breakfast. I am sure some of you will say, "What, onions for breakfast?" But this is a delicious dish, and especially popular in the wintertime.

As a girl, I was considered troubled. The problem was that I did not help around the house with cleaning or cooking. I was a tomboy who loved to play in the streets with my brothers, and I did very poorly at school. My mother decided I needed help to rid me of evil's spell. This entailed visiting "the witch," who my mother considered an expert on soul cleansing. The witch sat at a table talking what sounded like gibberish to me and spinning the round tabletop around and around. Inevitably, she would say, "This girl is cursed by the Devil! You need to come back many more times before I can cure her."

Our neighbour, Nasrat, had another idea, though. Just before dawn, while it was still pitch dark, Nasrat would pull me out of bed to catch the bus to a pond to talk directly to the Devil. We had to be by water for some reason. Maybe the Devil liked to swim at night? At the pond, I would kneel beside Nasrat and ask the Devil for forgiveness. Nasrat cried, prayed and pleaded for what felt like hours. Then she would convey the Devil's message to me, which was the same each time: that in order for me to be purified, I had to not touch a knife for a certain period, and there was to be no hopping, no eating certain foods, no jumping over a cat or even looking at a cat. The experience was frightening but I believed it—I didn't know any better. At least the ordeal always ended well: back home, while Nasrat reported on her conversation with the Devil, I would eat boiled onions and cheese from the pot.

You do not need to talk to the Devil in order to make or eat this dish. Use a hard Syrian, Lebanese or Iraqi cheese such as hallumi, or use Romano; the cheese must be hard enough to retain its firmness when cooked. Serve the onions with a few cubes of cheese in a warmed pita or eat on its own.

6 to 8 cups water, or more as needed

5 baby onions per person, or as many as desired

2 to 4 oz hard cheese (Romano or hallumi) per person, cubed

◇　◇　◇

1. Bring the water to a boil over high heat. Reduce the heat to medium, add the onions and cook for 20 minutes or until they are very tender. Add the cheese and cook for 5 minutes. Using a slotted spoon, transfer the onions and cheese to a serving plate.

POTATO LATKES WITH SPINACH AND FRESH HERBS

SABZI

Serves 6 to 8

3 potatoes

1 pkg (10 oz/284 g) fresh spinach, chopped

2 carrots, grated (optional)

1 bunch green onions, chopped

1 large onion, chopped

1 leek, well rinsed, finely chopped

1 bunch parsley, chopped

1 bunch coriander, chopped

½ lb ground beef, chicken or turkey (optional)

4 eggs

5 Tbsp all-purpose flour

2 tsp baking powder

1 Tbsp cumin

2 tsp pepper

1 tsp turmeric

salt

oil, for frying

My all-time favourite person, Nasrat, made this dish often. She lived behind our home in Israel in a house that had a tiny kitchen and a veranda shaded by the most beautiful cherry tree.

Blind in one eye, Nasrat was the sole breadwinner of her household. To support her children and husband, she plucked women's eyebrows and removed unwanted hair using a string. My dad told me that in Iran, Nasrat had gone into labour on her way to work, gave birth on a street corner, got up and went to work with the new-born. She had four children to feed and they had very little money, but the house was filled with love and laughter. I spent so much time there that I picked up Persian from her, and tasted many traditional Persian dishes.

When she cooked she sat on the floor, surrounded with greens, removing the stems and cleaning them. Next to her feet was a little gas burner. She had set up her work space outside on the veranda, and while she cooked, streams of women would come to have their hair removed. Nasrat would go back and forth, plucking hair and cooking.

After moving away, I went back to visit Nasrat several times. Each time, she had my favourite dishes waiting for me. The first time that I brought my husband and children along she started to sing my favourite songs for me. I turned to my daughter, who was then ten years old, and with tears in my eyes said, "Aren't these songs beautiful?" She replied, "I think you love Nasrat, not the songs."

The carrots in this dish are optional; they add a touch of sweetness.

1. Grate the potatoes, then squeeze to remove any excess water. Let drain in a strainer with a pinch of salt for 5 to 10 minutes.
2. In a bowl, combine all the latke ingredients, including the potatoes. Stir to mix well.
3. In a deep frying pan, heat the oil. Drop 1 to 2 tablespoonfuls of the mixture into the oil at a time. Cook until the latkes are browned. Remove from the oil with a slotted spoon and drain on a plate lined with paper towel. Use paper towel between each layer to drain.

VARIATIONS

To reduce the amount of oil used, do not fry individual latkes but instead cook the latke mixture in a deep frying pan with a little oil for 15 to 20 minutes over medium heat, stirring occasionally to prevent burning. Sprinkle with olive oil and place the pan in a 400°F oven for 1¼ to 1½ hours or until cooked in the centre. Or, bake the latkes on a baking sheet lined with parchment paper: Drop the latke mixture a couple of spoonfuls at a time onto the prepared baking sheet, pressing gently to flatten, and leaving a bit of space between each. Sprinkle with olive oil and bake in a 425°F oven for 20 to 25 minutes, until browned.

ZUCCHINI WITH RED LENTILS, GARLIC AND CUMIN

PILLAU BHEJAR

In the Middle East, people eat a lot of zucchini, often stuffed, or with meatballs. There are many varieties of zucchini, each with a slightly different taste. When I was growing up, I often saw women sitting on their verandas, bent over huge cast-iron bowls, scooping out the insides of tiny zucchini. Nowadays, in Arab markets, you can buy zucchini that are already hollowed out, ready to be stuffed.

My great-uncle loved this dish and requested it whenever he came to visit. He and his wife used to visit us often, staying with us for weeks at a time. I never knew that he was a very sick man because he never said anything about his illness, nor did he behave like a sick man. We only noticed that he ate very little but loved his zucchini stew, and that he drank tea and smoked non-stop. As kids we loved this uncle—he was magic. He would keep us up all night telling us stories—often one very long story that would continue each night and be completed on the last night he was there. When our parents and particularly his wife were asleep, he would take us to explore outdoors in the pitch dark and bring us all back just before sunrise.

We would do anything for him. In fact, we often fought among ourselves about who would be the one to fetch him whatever he asked for.

Iraqis often served this dish in the winter. The lentils add protein. I like to serve yogurt on the side.

1. Heat 2 Tbsp of the oil in a large, deep pot over low heat. Add the onion and garlic; sauté until light golden.
2. Stir in the tomato and simmer for 2 to 3 minutes.
3. Add the zucchini and parsley; sauté gently for 5 minutes.
4. Add the remaining ingredients, including the remaining 3 Tbsp oil, stirring well to mix.
5. Simmer, loosely covered, for 45 minutes, stirring occasionally. Taste the liquid occasionally to make sure there is enough cumin and garlic; add a little at a time as desired. The dish is cooked when the rice, lentils and zucchini are very soft and the rice still a bit moist.

VARIATION

Use rice only or lentils only, doubling the quantity called for.

Serves 4 to 6

5 Tbsp oil

1 large onion, chopped

1 head garlic, chopped

1 large tomato, chopped

4 zucchini, sliced into thin rounds

1 cup chopped parsley

1 cup long-grain white rice, soaked in cold water for 1 hour, then drained

½ cup red lentils, soaked in cold water for 1½ hours, then drained

1 can (5½ oz/156 mL) tomato paste

2 cubes chicken bouillon

2½ Tbsp cumin

1 Tbsp pepper

1 tsp turmeric

salt

boiling water, enough to cover the ingredients

Great-uncle Gorgy and his bride, Violet, Baghdad, c. 1940

Rice is to the Middle East what pasta is to Italy. While rice is a staple in Asian countries, there it is typically served plain, the flavours coming from the sauces for the vegetables, meat or legumes. Iraqi and particularly Iranian rice dishes, on the other hand, are known for their flavours, colours and, especially, their presentation. The way we serve them is something of a ritual. Having more than one rice dish at a meal is not unusual. Sometimes we even make a rice crust on the bottom of a dish so that, when served turned upside down, it looks like a cake.

It took me a long time to get used to making a smaller quantity of rice for dinner. When I was growing up, my mother would serve everyone a big mound of rice topped with whatever stew she had cooked that day. We'd eat the rice with a spoon or by scooping it up with a piece of hubus, or flatbread. I guarantee you that in any traditional Iranian home you'll find a huge pot of rice on the stove.

Recently I went to visit my old neighbour Nasrat, now in her mid-eighties. As soon as I sat down, Nasrat went to the kitchen and brought back out a plate of green rice with chicken and potatoes. I peeked into her kitchen and saw a huge pot of rice. "Nasrat, why do you cook so much?" I asked. She smiled and said, "You never know who comes through the door hungry."

RICE DISHES

Green Rice

SAFFRON RICE

Serves 4 to 6

4 Tbsp oil

1 onion, chopped

1½ cups rinsed basmati or long-
  grain white rice, soaked in
  cold water for 1 hour, then
  drained

1 cube chicken or vegetable
  bouillon

1 tsp pepper

5 to 6 threads saffron

water, enough to just cover rice
  (grains should be visible)

salt

When I first moved to Europe, I was served a meal with rice to eat with a fork and knife. For me, the easiest way to eat the rice was with the knife. I stacked the food on the knife and then stuck the knife in my mouth. When I thought no one was looking, I would pick up the food with my hand, especially if it was rice.

The Iranian and Iraqi method of preparing rice—partially cooking it, draining it, then returning it to the pot with fried onion and a touch of water and continuing to cook it very slowly—results in delicious dry, almost crispy, rice, but it is time-consuming and the rice loses some of its nutritional value. Here's my way.

1. In a pot, heat 1 to 2 Tbsp of the oil over low heat. Sauté the onion in the oil until light golden.
2. Add the rice and the remaining ingredients, including the remaining 2 to 3 Tbsp oil. Stir to mix well.
3. Bring the mixture to a boil, then reduce the heat to low. Taste the cooking liquid— the flavour should be strong, as it will mellow once the water evaporates. Add more salt, pepper or bouillon to taste.
4. Let cook, partially covered, until the water has evaporated. Reduce the heat and simmer, tightly covered, for 15 to 20 minutes. Remove the rice from the heat as soon as it is cooked and all the water has evaporated.

VARIATION

To jazz up the white rice, add ½ cup orzo. Sauté with the onion until light golden; continue as directed in the recipe.

GREEN RICE
PILLAU JORESH

This is one of my favourite rice dishes. When I left home at age fifteen, my dearest neighbour, Nasrat, made two dishes for me to take on the plane: green rice—*pillau joresh*—and beef and spinach stew, or *qormeh sabzi*. She put them in two small pots, stacked them one on top of the other, and wrapped them in a towel. When I arrived at Heathrow Airport in London, the immigration officer checked my passport, looked at me and pointed to the pots I was holding. I did not speak any English but figured that he wanted to see what I was carrying. I was excited; I pulled the lids off the pots and pushed them close to his mouth so he could have a taste. He jumped back, mortified.

If you want to have this rice dish as a complete meal with protein, opt for the lentils instead of the fava beans. I serve this dish with salad on the side. Iranians typically add sliced potatoes along with the onion when cooking, and serve the rice topped with crispy fried onions and the potatoes. It is the dill that makes this rice "green."

1. Heat 2 Tbsp of the oil over low heat. Fry the onion in the oil until light golden.
2. Stir in all of the remaining ingredients except for the lentils and bring to a boil. Reduce the heat to low and partially cover.
3. Just before all the water has evaporated, stir in the lentils. Taste the liquid; it should have a fairly strong flavour—it will weaken once the water evaporates. Adjust the dill, salt and pepper to taste. Stir in the remaining oil. Wrap the lid with a kitchen towel and replace on the pot tightly; this will absorb the moisture. Simmer for 10 to 15 minutes or until the rice is cooked.

Serves 6

5 Tbsp oil

1 onion, chopped

2 cups long-grain white rice, soaked in cold water for 1 hour, then drained

2 cubes chicken or vegetable bouillon

3 Tbsp dried dill or ½ bunch fresh dill, chopped

1 tsp turmeric

1 tsp pepper

salt

water, enough to just cover rice (grains should be visible)

1 can (19 oz/540 mL) brown lentils or small green fava beans, rinsed and drained, or 2 cups cooked dried brown lentils (see page 156)

FESTIVE RICE

Serves 4 to 6

Rice Mixture

5 Tbsp oil

1 large onion, chopped

2 cups long-grain white rice, soaked in cold water for 1 hour, then drained

½ cup finely chopped parsley

3 Tbsp tomato paste

2 cubes chicken or vegetable bouillon

1 tsp pepper

1 tsp turmeric

⅛ tsp saffron threads, steeped in 2 Tbsp hot water

salt

water, enough to just cover rice (grains should be visible)

Garnish

½ cup raisins, plus more for sprinkling

½ cup slivered almonds, plus more for sprinkling

2 Tbsp oil

At one time it was Iraqi tradition that when a woman had a baby boy, she became a big star. She would lie in bed for forty days, wearing beautifully embroidered dresses and being waited upon. In fact, she was not allowed to go out. People visited and brought her goodies. When the infant's nails were cut for the first time, at around one month, the nails were added to a rice dish topped with roasted almonds and raisins and shared among relatives, friends and neighbours. I still like to cook festive rice from time to time, but without the baby nails.

The rice will keep in the refrigerator for at least 2 days. I sometimes freeze leftovers in a resealable bag. This rice dish goes well with many of the stews, especially the eggplant, okra or apricot.

◈　◈　◈

1. Heat 2 Tbsp of the oil in a pot over medium heat. Add the onion and sauté until golden.
2. Add the remaining rice mixture ingredients, including the remaining 3 Tbsp oil and the saffron with its soaking water. Stir to mix well.
3. Bring the mixture to a boil, then reduce the heat to low and cover loosely. When almost all the water has evaporated, stir and adjust seasonings to taste. Cover tightly and simmer for 10 to 15 minutes.
4. Meanwhile, *to prepare the garnish,* in a frying pan, sauté the raisins and almonds with 2 Tbsp oil, until light golden.
5. Serve the rice on a flat serving platter, sprinkled with the raisins and almonds.

RICE WITH CARROTS, ALMONDS AND RAISINS

Some of the villages in and around Darjeeling, in India, are almost impossible to reach except by foot. The village of Ambutia, about five hours from Darjeeling by foot, is a dreamlike place, a never-never land with the most beautiful flowers, plants and trees imaginable. There is no electricity and no cars or even bicycles. The only sounds are of people, birds, wind and water.

But beautiful scenery alone can't feed people. For decades, Ambutia was a tea garden. When the owners abandoned the land, the village turned into a wasteland. Nothing could grow in the exhausted soil, and the one-crop economy had left the people with no sustaining crops. Starvation and malnutrition were rampant, and many people lived in subhuman conditions. In 1969, Father Burns, along with a volunteer group from St. Joseph's College in Darjeeling, assisted the villagers with medical and educational support and, most importantly, helped them cultivate their land. The village was transformed into a well-run, self-sufficient and contented community. All the food in Ambutia is from the land and prepared by the villagers. They also run a milk co-op.

I was there in the late 1990s working on a series of radio documentaries about the work of the Jesuits in that part of the world. I spent some time with two young men who ran the milk co-op, and who would walk to the market in Darjeeling to sell their products. These two men were the most contented human beings I've ever met. I asked one of them, "You smile and sing all day long; why are you so happy?" He smiled and said, "What's not to smile about? My parents were starving to death, and now my family and I are well fed. We cultivate our land, milk our cows collectively, and I have a beautiful wife and two beautiful children …" He burst into a song he serenades his wife with. The men then insisted I share their lunch with them. Over a little fire, they heated up a pot with some rice and vegetables. How simple but delicious it was.

This rice dish is not as simple but it is equally delicious.

1. In a pot over medium heat, sauté the onion with 2 Tbsp of the oil until golden.
2. Add the carrots, raisins and almonds; sauté for 3 to 4 minutes.
3. Add the remaining ingredients, including the remaining 3 Tbsp oil and the saffron with its soaking water. Stir to mix well.
4. Bring the mixture to a boil, then reduce the heat to low and cover loosely. When the water has almost evaporated, stir and season to taste. Cover tightly and reduce the heat to low; simmer for 20 to 25 minutes, or until the rice is cooked.

Serves 4 to 6

1 large onion, chopped

5 Tbsp oil or butter

1½ cups grated carrot

1 cup raisins, plus more to taste

1 cup slivered almonds, plus more to taste

2 cups long-grain white rice, soaked in cold water for 1 hour, then drained

grated peel of 1 orange

juice of 1 orange

2 cubes chicken or vegetable bouillon

1 tsp turmeric

1 tsp pepper

⅛ tsp saffron threads, steeped in 2 Tbsp hot water

salt

water, enough to just cover rice (grains should be visible)

RICE WITH CHERRIES AND SAFFRON

Serves 4 to 6

1 large onion, chopped

5 Tbsp oil or butter

grated peel of 1 orange

1 cup dried cherries

2 cups long-grain white rice, soaked in cold water for 1 hour, then drained

2 cubes chicken or vegetable bouillon

3 Tbsp sugar (optional)

⅛ tsp saffron threads, steeped in 2 Tbsp hot water

salt and pepper

water, enough to just cover rice (grains should be visible)

I was in Nepal with a team of volunteer healthcare workers who provided basic medical services in remote villages. In the first village we visited, the volunteers set up in a modest two-room schoolhouse. Before long, there was a huge lineup of people—young and old—waiting to see the doctor. According to the doctor, many people in the region suffered from severe respiratory problems.

I walked around the village and talked to the locals through a translator. Most owned small plots of land, and their main crop was rice. One woman invited me to her home. She looked old and had a married daughter, but she was only in her mid-thirties. She told me that she was very upset with her daughter because her daughter's husband had sent her back home. "The mother-in-law did not like my daughter," she said. "My daughter did not work hard enough. We had to pay to marry her off and now she is back at home with a baby. We are poor and cannot afford to feed my daughter and granddaughter."

As the mother spoke, the daughter stood there holding her baby and hanging her head. I don't think she was more than sixteen. She was a stunning-looking woman but with the saddest face. This young woman then took me to the fields and explained the planting of rice. I asked her what had really happened to her. She told me that her mother-in-law and her husband had beaten her regularly. They believed that her parents had not given them enough dowry and that they could have done better with another family. She bent down, picked a rice stump and blew the shell. Looking at me she said, "I am a big burden on my parents, but I prefer to stay with them than with my in-laws." I wanted to embrace her and say, "Do not worry, everything will be okay."

Even though this rice recipe is an Iranian one, I dedicate it to that young Nepalese woman. She was as sweet, if not sweeter, than this dish. This Iranian sweet rice dish is very festive.

◇　◇　◇

NOTE: I like to reserve 2 Tbsp of the oil to sauté the rice in after the water has been absorbed and the rice is cooked.

1. In a pot over medium heat, sauté the onion with 2 Tbsp of the oil until light golden.
2. Reduce the heat to medium-low and add the orange peel and cherries. Sauté for 3 to 4 minutes.
3. Add the remaining ingredients, including the saffron with its soaking water. Stir to mix well.
4. Bring the mixture to a boil. Loosely cover the pot and reduce the heat to low; simmer until the water has been absorbed and the rice is cooked, about 20 to 25 minutes. Season with more salt and pepper to taste.

RICE WITH RED LENTILS AND CUMIN
KETCHRI

When I was growing up in Israel, my family ate this dish every Thursday. My dad told us that when he grew up in Iraq, his mother, too, made *ketchri* every Thursday. I'm not sure why Thursdays. What can I tell you about this dish? It is smooth, with a fantastic fragrance from the cumin and garlic. I always make extra to give to my neighbours and friends. I make it as a main course and serve it with Green Salad with Lemon Garlic Dressing (page 26) or with Cabbage Salad with Zesty Mint Dressing (page 31), with plain yogurt on the side. As a treat, I'll gently stir small cubes of feta cheese into the rice just before serving.

1. Pick over the lentils for small stones, then rinse well and soak in cold water with the rice for 1 hour.
2. In a heavy-bottomed pot over low heat, sauté the onion and garlic in 2 Tbsp of the oil until light golden.
3. Drain the rice and lentils, and add to the pot along with the remaining ingredients. Stir to mix well.
4. Bring the mixture to a boil, then reduce the heat to low and cover the pot halfway. Just before the water has all been absorbed, stir and taste—you should be able to taste the garlic, cumin and other spices. Add more, a little at a time, to taste. Cover the pot tightly and simmer for 25 to 35 minutes or until the rice and lentils are soft.

Serves 4 to 6

1 cup red lentils

1 cup long-grain white rice

1 large onion, chopped

1 head garlic, chopped

5 Tbsp oil

2 cubes vegetable or chicken bouillon

3 Tbsp tomato paste

2 Tbsp cumin

1 Tbsp garlic powder (optional)

1 Tbsp pepper

1 tsp turmeric

salt

water, enough to generously cover rice and lentils

RICE CHIAPAS STYLE

Serves 4 to 6

5 Tbsp oil

2 onions, chopped

1 head garlic, chopped

2 ripe tomatoes, chopped

1 red pepper, chopped

1 cup chopped parsley

½ cup chopped mushrooms

1 tsp pepper or chopped
  jalapeño pepper (remove
  seeds for less heat)

2 cups long-grain white rice,
  soaked in cold water for
  1 hour, then drained

2 cubes vegetable bouillon

3 Tbsp tomato paste

1 tsp turmeric

salt

water, enough to just cover rice
  (grains should be visible)

1 can (19 oz/540 mL) red kidney
  or black beans, drained and
  rinsed, or 2 cups cooked
  dried beans (see page 156)

The first time I had this rice dish was in Chiapas, the southern state of Mexico, where I was for my documentary series on indigenous people around the world. It was in the mid-1990s, during the civil war between the Mexican army and the landless indigenous population led by the Zapatistas. I had joined the observers—human rights activists, church leaders and students—who had come together from all over Mexico and other Latin American countries in solidarity with the peasants of Chiapas. We travelled at night on dirt roads from San Cristobal, the capital of Chiapas, deep into *la selva*, the forest. We were there to monitor and report on the destruction of homes, fields and livestock, and on the economic repercussions and cruelty inflicted by the army on the poor peasants. I saw despair, fear and panic rampant among the peasants.

One day an older man joined us. He brought with him a little pot of rice and beans that he insisted we share with him. As we ate, he told us his story: his house had been destroyed and his fields burned, and his son had disappeared. When I asked if he dreamed of revenge, he looked at me and said in a quiet voice, "If I go that route, I will be just like the soldiers who are destroying our lives …"

Later, I returned to San Cristobal to join the convoy to Mexico City. But that night there was a huge mass, led by Bishop Samuel Aroz. There had been threats to his life by the right-wing militia. As a result, peasants from all over the region were coming to San Cristobal to protect him and defend the cathedral, encircling it with a human chain. And that night in particular the organizers believed the militia would attack and were pleading with journalists and human rights activists to stay, thinking the militia would be less likely to attack in the presence of journalists and foreigners. During his sermon, the bishop talked about the need for justice for the poor, but even more interesting was the message of forgiveness rather than hatred for the soldiers; they too, he said, came from simple backgrounds.

I later joined the convoy of thousands of peasants, human rights activists and volunteers from Chiapas to the capital, Mexico City, with a message of peace and to let the government and the people of Mexico hear our concerns. The convoy stopped in small towns along the way for rallies. People came out in solidarity and gave the peasants whatever they could afford. I never before had felt so deeply a part of a cause. When we arrived in Mexico City and marched to the legislature, hundreds of thousands of people came out to greet us, to chant with us and to toss flowers to us. The welcome was overwhelming.

On the road, we ate at almost every meal a mix of greens. We dipped our hands into bags filled with coriander, green onions and jalapeño peppers, eating it from our hands. There was also always a huge pot of rice. The women cooked the meals in big pots over little gas heaters. Everyone did their share to prepare the meals, then waited their turn to eat—and the children never asked for a second helping. And the rice and beans they made tasted so good. I hope this recipe does justice to the experience I had in Mexico.

◇　◇　◇

1. In a pot, heat 2 Tbsp of the oil over low heat. Sauté the onions and garlic until light golden.
2. Add the tomatoes, red pepper, parsley, mushrooms and pepper. Stir to mix, then simmer for 3 to 4 minutes.
3. Add all of the remaining ingredients (including the remaining 3 Tbsp oil), except for the beans. Cover loosely, bring to a boil, then reduce the heat to low. Stir and season with salt and pepper.
4. Stir in the beans. Simmer for 20 to 25 minutes or until the rice is cooked.

VARIATION

Omit the beans and instead use 2 cups combination of white and wild rice (presoaked in cold water for 1 to 2 hours). Add ½ cup chopped sun-dried tomatoes and ½ cup pine nuts. Generously cover the rice with water (approximately 4 to 5 cups) and simmer for 35 to 45 minutes.

Chiapas, Mexico, 2005

Growing up in an Iraqi home, I ate predominantly vegetable stews mixed with a little meat or chicken. Later upon travelling and living in parts of the world where the majority of people are destitute, I found that there too most of the dishes are predominantly vegetable, with just a little meat or with legumes.

These stews are not complicated or expensive, but they are full of flavour. When I go grocery shopping, I think of what vegetable stews I am going to make—celery with mint, or green beans with parsley, or sweet-and-sour okra with coriander—then buy a little meat or chicken to add in.

STEWS

Sweet-and-Sour Squash with Raisins and Meatballs

SWEET-AND-SOUR APRICOT STEW

Serves 6

4 Tbsp olive oil

1 large onion, finely chopped

2 large tomatoes, chopped

2 stalks celery, chopped

1 green pepper, finely chopped

1 bunch green onions, finely chopped

1 bunch parsley, finely chopped

2 lb stewing beef or boneless chicken breast, cut into chunks

2 cups dried apricots, chopped

1 can (14 oz/398 mL) tomato sauce

½ cup fresh lemon juice, plus more as needed

2 cubes chicken bouillon

3 Tbsp ketchup (optional)

1 tsp turmeric

1 tsp pepper

salt

5 cups water (or enough to cover ingredients)

Variation: Meatballs

1½ lb ground beef, chicken or turkey

1 medium onion, finely chopped

1 bunch parsley, finely chopped

1 egg

4 Tbsp dried bread crumbs

1 Tbsp cumin

½ Tbsp pepper

1 tsp turmeric

salt

For my boyfriend's birthday—we were in graduate school together—I wanted to make something special to impress him, but I was very nervous about feeding a fruit-and-meat dish to a meat-and-potatoes guy from Alberta. When Bernie first saw the dish, a look of panic crossed his face. He was polite enough not to say anything, but he didn't have to—his facial expression said it all. To calm him down, I told him, "Just try the dish. If you hate it, we can order Chinese." Putting the first bite into his mouth, it was as if it were a spoonful of cod liver oil. But he loved it. Bernie is now my husband and, since then, I have always made this dish for his birthday. I must confess that he is the greatest fan of my cooking. And he has almost forgotten the meat-and-potatoes dishes he grew up on.

I serve this stew with red or white rice and a salad. It's a filling dish because of the apricots.

1. Heat the oil in a large pot over low heat. Sauté the onion in the oil until light golden.
2. Add the tomatoes, celery, green pepper, green onions and parsley; cook for 5 minutes.
3. Increase the heat to medium, add the meat and sauté for 7 to 10 minutes. (If preparing the meatball variation below, add the meatballs at this point.)
4. Add the remaining ingredients, stirring well to mix.
5. Bring the mixture to a boil, then reduce the heat to low and simmer for 1½ to 2 hours, partially covered, until the meat is tender and cooked through and the sauce is slightly thickened and very flavourful. Halfway through cooking, taste the sauce; it should be sweet and sour. If it is too sweet, add more lemon juice; if it is too sour, add sugar, a little at a time. If the sauce is too thick, add a little water.

VARIATION

Make as directed, but instead of sautéing chunks of beef or chicken in Step 3, use meatballs.

1. In a bowl, combine the meatball ingredients.
2. Place the meatball mixture and another bowl filled with cold water next to the stove.
3. Using the palms of your hands moistened with the cold water, shape the mixture into balls the size of walnuts, dropping them one by one into the onion-tomato mixture as they are formed.
4. Once the meatballs are partially cooked, continue with Step 4 above.

IRAQI GREEN BEAN STEW

When I was a child, we ate green bean stew in winter, and for me, it is a comfort food. It is a typical everyday dish in both poor and wealthy Iraqi households.

I have a very vivid memory of this dish being fed to my older brother while he was extremely sick with thrombosis. He was about sixteen, and I remember him lying on a wooden bench in the room screaming from pain. My mother called in the witch doctor, believing she would have the power to heal David. I could hear my brother screaming "Stop it! Stop it!" The witch doctor was pulling his leg. My dad had enough sense to call the local doctor, who called an ambulance. David stayed in the hospital for quite a while, and the only thing he would eat was green bean stew.

1. In a large pot, heat the oil over low heat. Add the onion and garlic; sauté until light golden.
2. Add the tomatoes; cook for 3 to 5 minutes.
3. Add the meat. Increase the heat to medium and sauté for 7 to 10 minutes, stirring occasionally to prevent sticking.
4. Add the remaining ingredients and bring to a gentle boil, again stirring to prevent sticking.
5. Reduce the heat and simmer for about 50 or 60 minutes, partially covered, until the vegetables and meat are very tender. If the water evaporates, add more, about ½ cup at a time.
6. Before serving, adjust seasonings, adding more salt, pepper and herbs to taste.

VARIATION

For Palestinian style, add 1 Tbsp cinnamon and 1 Tbsp allspice along with the other spices.

Serves 6

4 Tbsp oil

1 large onion, finely chopped

1 head garlic, chopped

2 ripe tomatoes, chopped

2 lb boneless, skinless chicken breast or stewing beef, cut into small strips

2 lb fresh beans, trimmed, or frozen beans (preferably thinly sliced)

2 small carrots, thinly sliced (optional)

1 bunch parsley, finely chopped

5 cups water (or enough to cover ingredients)

1 can (14 oz/398 mL) tomato sauce

2 cubes chicken bouillon

2 tsp pepper

1 tsp turmeric

salt

GREEN FAVA BEANS WITH BEEF, LIME AND MINT

Serves 6

1 large onion, finely chopped

1 head garlic, chopped

4 Tbsp olive oil

2 tomatoes, chopped

1½ lb lean stewing beef or
½ medium whole chicken,
skinned and cut into 6 pieces

2 lb small green fava beans,
frozen or canned

5 cups water (or enough to cover
ingredients)

1 can (14 oz/398 mL) tomato
sauce

½ cup fresh lime juice

2 cubes chicken or vegetable
bouillon

4 Tbsp dried mint

2 tsp pepper

1 tsp turmeric

salt

Salja, an old neighbour in Israel, cooked this stew frequently on her little gas camping stove. From the age of eight until my early teens, I loved going to her house after school to see what she was cooking. Like most women of her generation, she started cooking the meal of the day early in the morning, to be ready for lunch. When I stopped by her house, she would serve me lunch no matter how little she had, sharing it between me and her own child. I also loved visiting her because she told us funny stories she had heard in the market, or would share with us the latest prediction from the fortune teller. I must admit, I went to the same fortune teller almost as often as Salja did. The fortune teller always told me the same thing: "You will get a letter from far away; there are bumps on the way and you will go to faraway places." Her prediction was music to my ears.

With this recipe I hope to come as close as possible to Salja's. I serve this stew on white or red rice. I make it regularly and, like all the stews in this book, this one stretches quite a bit. You can freeze any leftovers.

1. In a large pot over low heat, sauté the onion and garlic in the oil until light golden.
2. Add the tomatoes and simmer for 2 to 3 minutes, covered.
3. Increase the heat to medium-low, add the meat and sauté 5 to 7 minutes.
4. Add the remaining ingredients, stirring to mix well.
5. Bring the mixture to a low boil. Reduce the heat and let simmer, partially covered and stirring occasionally, for about 1 hour. After about 20 minutes, adjust seasonings, including lime juice, to taste. The flavour should be of mint and lime but not too sour.

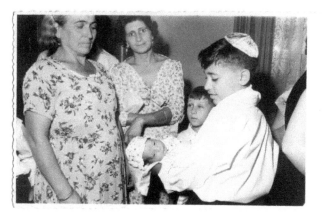

Salja (left), Ramat Gan, Israel, *c.* 1958

SWEET-AND-SOUR OKRA STEW

Okra may be an acquired taste. But give it a chance, because it is a healthy and versatile vegetable. Okra is popular in the Middle East and in some parts of Africa, Asia, the Caribbean, the southern United States and the Mediterranean. When I spent time in Greece, I often ate okra with tomato sauce as a side dish.

In the summer months in the Middle East, the women in my neighbourhood used a needle and thread to hang fresh okra on a washing line to dry. We ate okra at least once a week. Now I usually cook with it in the winter, buying it frozen. Pomegranate molasses, also called pomegranate syrup or concentrate, is sold at Middle Eastern food stores and some supermarkets. I serve this stew over white or red rice.

NOTE: If making the meatball variation below, begin by preparing the meatball mixture, so that it is ready to add to the tomato mixture in Step 3.

1. In a deep pot over low heat, heat the oil and add the onion and garlic. Sauté until light golden.
2. Add the tomatoes, celery and parsley; stir for 3 to 4 minutes.
3. Increase the heat to medium, add the meat and sauté, stirring to prevent sticking on the bottom, for 3 to 4 minutes, until partially cooked. (If preparing the meatball variation below, add the meatballs at this point.)
4. Add the okra.
5. In a bowl, combine the sauce ingredients. Gently stir into the okra mixture.
6. Increase the heat slightly and bring the stew to a boil, continuing to stir gently to prevent sticking or burning. Once the mixture has come to a boil, reduce the heat and simmer for 1 to 1½ hours, partially covered, until the meat and okra are very tender. Taste occasionally during cooking, adding more water, lemon juice or other seasonings to taste, a little at a time. The stew should have a gentle lemon flavour, with a touch of sweetness from the herbs.

VARIATION

Make as directed, but instead of sautéing chunks of beef or chicken in Step 3, use meatballs.

1. In a bowl, combine the meatball ingredients.
2. Place the meatball mixture and another bowl filled with cold water next to the stove.
3. Using the palms of your hands moistened with the cold water, shape the mixture into balls the size of walnuts, dropping them one by one into the onion-tomato mixture as they are formed.
4. Once the meatballs are partially cooked, add the okra (Step 4 above) and continue as directed.

Serves 4 to 6

4 Tbsp oil

1 large onion, sliced

1 head garlic, sliced

2 large ripe tomatoes, thinly sliced

2 stalks celery, thinly sliced (leaves included)

1 bunch parsley or coriander, chopped

12 fresh mint leaves, chopped

2 lb stewing beef or boneless, skinless chicken, cut into chunks

2 pkgs (10 oz/300 g each) frozen okra or 2 lb fresh okra, trimmed

Sauce

5 cups water (or enough to just cover ingredients)

1 can (14 oz/398 mL) tomato sauce or 1 can (5½ oz/ 156 mL) tomato paste

juice of 2 lemons

2 cubes chicken bouillon

2 Tbsp pomegranate molasses (optional)

1 Tbsp sugar

2 tsp pepper

1 tsp turmeric

salt

Variation: Meatballs

1½ lb ground beef, chicken or turkey

1 medium onion, finely chopped

1 bunch parsley, finely chopped

1 egg

4 Tbsp dried bread crumbs

1 Tbsp cumin

½ Tbsp pepper

1 tsp turmeric

salt

SIMMERED CABBAGE STEW WITH CHICKEN

Serves 4 to 6

4 Tbsp oil

1 large onion, sliced

1 head garlic, chopped

½ medium whole chicken (with
    or without skin), cut into
    pieces (or the equivalent in
    any chicken parts), or 1 beef
    shank bone

1 cabbage, sliced

4 cups water

2 carrots, quartered

2 potatoes, cubed

1 bunch parsley, chopped

4 bay leaves

2 cubes chicken bouillon

2 tsp pepper or 1 jalapeño
    pepper, chopped (remove
    seeds for less heat)

salt

I love the light sweetness of this earthy-tasting dish. At one point I lived in Montreal in a rundown rooming house with a shared bathroom. Each room had a bed, a small table and two chairs and a tiny hot plate. Two prostitutes and an older couple on disability assistance lived on my floor. There was quite a bit of screaming, yelling and violence on my floor from the drunken customers who visited the prostitutes. I used to be so afraid that I never left my room at night, not even to go to the bathroom. I even put my bed against my door to block it. Despite all this, there was a lot of camaraderie among us, and we helped each other as much as we could.

Once a month when the elderly couple's disability cheque arrived, they made a big batch of cabbage stew with a few chicken wings and necks and called us in to share the meal and watch TV with them. I loved these occasions, and the couple became family to me. They were very generous with the little they had. They even kept a bowl of bonbons on the table. The one Christmas we spent together, Maria knit scarves for me and the two other women. What a beautiful gift! So I always think of this cabbage dish with love.

1. In a deep pot, heat the oil over low heat. Sauté the onion and garlic until light golden. Continue to cook for 3 to 5 minutes.
2. Increase the heat to medium-low. Add the meat and sauté for a few minutes, until partially cooked.
3. Add the cabbage and 1 cup of the water.
4. Let the stew reduce a little, then add the remaining ingredients, including the remaining 3 cups water.
5. Increase the heat to medium-high and bring the stew to a boil, stirring often to prevent burning on the bottom. Reduce the heat and simmer for 1 to 1½ hours, partially covered, until the vegetables and meat are tender and flavourful. Check every 20 minutes or so, adjusting the seasonings to taste. If the stew is too thick, add more water, a little at a time.

SPICED CABBAGE AND MEAT STEW

I find it so remarkable that when travelling far from our own milieus, we are often much more open to meeting and talking to strangers than usual. In Kathmandu, Nepal, where I was making documentaries, I spent a few days in a hotel that had many foreign guests, of all ages and nationalities. On my second night there, I went to the hotel patio restaurant for dinner, finding a table among the guests already there. That evening we each began our meals at our separate tables, but gradually we started to talk to each other, and move our chairs closer and closer together.

Among the guests was a Belgian couple, both writers, who had travelled in their car across Europe and then Asia. As we ate, we tried to come up with an idea for their new novel. Another couple was from the United States and had just spent two years in Africa. The French surgeon was trying to find himself, so we attempted to help him, but to no avail. The Japanese businessman was extremely reserved at first, but by the end of the evening he was practically kissing us all. And the retired English nurse, who appeared shy, had in fact led a wild life. And, finally, there was me. I considered myself the most "normal" of the bunch!

We ended up spending the evening together, laughing and talking about life. We sat there until the early hours of the morning, ordering food whenever we felt hungry again. At one point, I ordered a very hearty rich cabbage dish. This dish is as hearty, though not as rich, as the one I had in Kathmandu. I serve it over white rice.

1. In a large pot, sauté the onion and garlic in the oil over low heat until light golden.
2. Add the ground meat. Increase the heat to medium and stir continuously until the meat is partially cooked, 3 to 4 minutes.
3. Gradually stir in the cabbage, 2 cups at a time, covering the pot between batches to allow the cabbage to wilt (it will take 3 to 5 minutes for each batch).
4. Add the water, bouillon cubes and spices, stirring to mix well.
5. Simmer for 50 to 60 minutes, partially covered, until the cabbage is tender. After about 25 minutes, adjust seasonings to taste; you should be able to taste the allspice. Add more water, a little at a time, if the stew is too thick.
6. Meanwhile, toast the pine nuts on a baking sheet in a 350°F oven or on the stovetop in a heavy frying pan for 3 to 5 minutes or until lightly golden. Watch them carefully—they burn quickly.
7. When the stew is cooked, stir in the toasted pine nuts and serve.

Serves 4 to 6

1 large onion, chopped

1 head garlic, chopped

3 Tbsp oil

1½ lb ground beef, chicken or turkey

1 cabbage, finely sliced

2 cups water

2 cubes chicken bouillon

2 Tbsp allspice

1 Tbsp pepper

salt

½ cup pine nuts

SWEET-AND-SOUR BEETS WITH SPICED MEATBALLS

KIBBAA BEL SHELRAAM

Serves 6 to 8

Meatballs

2 lb ground beef, chicken or turkey

1 large onion, finely chopped

1 bunch parsley, chopped

1 egg

5 Tbsp dried bread crumbs (optional)

4 Tbsp cold water, plus more as needed

1½ Tbsp each allspice and cinnamon

1 Tbsp each pepper, garlic powder and cumin

½ Tbsp each ground cloves and nutmeg

salt

Stew

4 Tbsp oil

2 large onions, finely chopped

5 medium beets, peeled and cubed

1 bunch parsley, finely chopped

½ cup fresh lemon juice

2 cubes chicken bouillon

2 Tbsp sugar

2 Tbsp each allspice and cinnamon

1 Tbsp each nutmeg and pepper

salt

water, enough to generously cover ingredients

When I think of beets, or *shelraam,* I think of winter—cold outdoors but warm indoors. For me, this dish is an absolute must to make. I make it on the weekends, when I have time to slice the beets (although I am sometimes too lazy to peel them and instead just scrub them well) and let them simmer for a long time—it takes a while for the beets to soften and release their sweetness. This dish is typically Iraqi, though traditionally it's made in a more elaborate way, by covering the meatballs in a ground rice shell, or *kibbaa*. I prefer to make small regular meatballs.

Cars were not part of our lives when I was growing up in Israel, and when we visited relatives, as we often did, we took the bus. About once a month we visited my Auntie Haanini, who lived some distance away. By car the trip would likely have taken only about 20 minutes, but because the buses did not run frequently and we had to transfer a few times, we would often be waiting at bus stops for what amounted to hours. So we took lunch and snacks with us and hoped that by evening we would reach our destination.

My aunt looked ancient to me, though she was probably only fifty; it was her hard life that made her look older. She always wore a thick grey headscarf that came down over her forehead and a long grey dress like that of a nun or traditional Arab. She had dressed in this fashion since her husband died. She lived with her two sons in a one-room apartment. In the tiny kitchen she kept bundles of roasted watermelon seeds, rice and homemade baking wrapped in fabric. When we arrived, we would run to her kitchen and anxiously wait for her to open these "treasure bags" to see what kinds of goodies she pulled out.

Without fail, she made this beet dish, *shelraam,* for us. I felt like I was in heaven sitting around the little Hibachi, the fragrance of smouldering orange peels filling the air, eating *shelraam* and listening to my mother and aunt gossip. And they always found something to cry about. In fact, I remember my mother keeping a handkerchief pinned to her dress just in case she cried and needed to blow her nose.

I cannot imagine this beet dish making anyone cry; in fact, I can almost guarantee anyone who tastes it will love it. Serve with white rice, and freeze any leftovers, if you like.

◇　◇　◇

1. *To prepare the meatballs,* in a deep large bowl, combine the meatball ingredients. Using your hands, mix well, continuously moistening your hands and sprinkling the ingredients with cold water, adding about 1 Tbsp at a time, to help bind the ingredients. To test that the seasoning is right, bake a small amount of the mixture in a toaster oven or cook in the microwave, then sample—it should have a touch of allspice and cinnamon; add more spices to taste.

2. Set the mixture and a small bowl of cold water next to the stove.

3. *To prepare the stew,* heat the oil in a large soup pot over low heat. Add the onions and cook until light golden. Increase the heat to medium.

4. Using the palms of your hands moistened with the cold water, shape the meatball mixture into small balls about the size of walnuts. Drop into the pot one by one as they are formed. (If you are not using bread crumbs, the meatball mixture will not shape firmly; just drop walnut-size portions into the pot without attempting to make perfectly round balls.)

5. When the meatballs are partially cooked, add the remaining stew ingredients to the pot, stirring to mix well. Make sure that the meatballs do not stick to the bottom and that they are generously covered with water. Increase the heat to high and bring the stew to a boil, loosely covered.

6. Reduce the heat to simmer; cook for at least 2 to 2½ hours, partially covered and stirring occasionally, until the beets are tender and the flavours have developed— the stew should have a sweet-and-sour flavour. If it is too sweet, add more lemon juice and spices. Add water as necessary to keep the vegetables and meatballs covered.

Auntie Haanini (centre, in scarf), Israel, c. 1958

SWEET-AND-SOUR CELERY WITH MIND AND LEMON

KHORESH KARAFS

Serves 4 to 6

1 large onion, chopped

1 head garlic, chopped

4 Tbsp oil

1 large ripe tomato, chopped

½ medium whole chicken, skinned and quartered (or the equivalent in any chicken parts), or 1½ lb stewing beef

1 bunch celery, thinly sliced (leaves included)

2 carrot, sliced (optional)

1 can (5½ oz/156 mL) tomato paste or 1 can (14 oz/398 mL) tomato sauce

¼ cup fresh lemon juice

2 cubes chicken bouillon

4 Tbsp dried mint

3 Tbsp ketchup (optional)

1 Tbsp sugar

2 tsp pepper

1 tsp turmeric

salt

water, enough to cover ingredients

Variation: Meatballs

1½ lb ground beef, chicken or turkey

1 large onion, very finely chopped

1 bunch parsley, finely chopped

1 egg

5 Tbsp dried bread crumbs

5 Tbsp cold water

1 Tbsp each allspice and cinnamon

1 Tbsp pepper

1 tsp turmeric

salt

The first time I had this Iranian celery stew was in Montreal at a relative's house—I called her "aunt," even though she wasn't really. From time to time this aunt would invite me over and give me some of her old clothes and food to take home. And often she would make this dish, which I always loved. With a little modification, I came up with this version, which is less sweet and has more mint than my aunt's. I serve this stew with white or red rice.

◈　◈　◈

NOTE: If making the meatball variation below, begin by preparing the meatball mixture, so that it is ready to add to the tomato mixture in Step 3.

1. In a large, deep pot over low heat, sauté the onion and garlic in the oil until light golden.
2. Add the tomato and sauté for 3 to 5 minutes.
3. Increase the heat to medium-low. Add the chicken and sauté for 7 to 10 minutes. (Or, if preparing the meatball variation below, add the meatballs at this point.)
4. Add the remaining ingredients, stirring to prevent sticking on the bottom.
5. Bring the mixture to a boil, then reduce the heat and simmer for 45 to 60 minutes, partially covered, until the meat and vegetables are very tender. Halfway through cooking, taste and adjust the salt, pepper, lemon juice, mint and liquid. The stew should have a slight lemon and definite mint flavour, with a touch of sweetness.

VARIATION

Make as directed, but instead of using chicken or beef, make meatballs.

1. In a bowl, and using your hands constantly moistened with cold water, combine the meatball ingredients, including the 5 Tbsp of water.
2. Set the mixture and a bowl of cold water next to the stove.
3. Using the palms of your hands and dipping your hands continuously into the cold water, shape the mixture into balls the size of walnuts, dropping each into the onion-tomato mixture as it is formed. Shake the pot to prevent the balls from sticking to the bottom.
4. Continue as directed (Steps 4 and 5 above).

BAKED CELERY WITH CHICKEN, DILL AND CORIANDER

In 1975, while I was working at the McGill University library in Montreal, I went to New York for a weekend to visit relatives. Upon hearing that I was going, the librarian asked me to get her the Black Panthers' newsletter. I said sure, unaware that the Black Panthers was an outlaw group considered a criminal organization in the United States. In Brooklyn, I stopped the first police officer I saw and said, "Excuse me, sir, do you know where I can buy the Black Panthers' newsletter?"

I was with my aunt, who was as ignorant as I was about politics. She smiled and said, "Let's go home to eat my delicious baked celery dish. We will go after dinner to ask the man who sells newspapers at the corner of our street."

The juices and herbs make this tasty dish soothing, with a fantastic aroma. The carrots are optional; they add sweetness. Once again, since it is a stew, it goes a long way. Make this stew for a party, or portion it out for a couple of meals. Serve with Saffron Rice (page 76) or Green Rice (page 77).

1. In a large bowl, combine all the ingredients except for the chicken and water. Taste the mixture to make sure it has a strong lemon and herb flavour, adding more lemon juice and herbs as needed.
2. Place the chicken in a deep ovenproof dish (clay is best). Top with the vegetable mixture and pour in the water.
3. Bake in a 425°F oven for 1½ hours, uncovered, or until the chicken is cooked through and the vegetables are tender. Halfway through cooking, baste the chicken and taste the liquid. Add more lemon juice and other seasonings to taste. Add more water if needed to keep the stew moist.

Serves 4 to 6

2 carrots, sliced (optional)

1 bunch celery, finely chopped (leaves included)

1 green or red pepper, sliced

1 bunch green onions, sliced

1 large onion, chopped

1 head garlic, chopped

1 small pkg frozen peas (approx 2 cups)

½ bunch each coriander, parsley and dill, finely chopped

1 cup pitted green or black olives, sliced

½ cup fresh lemon juice

3 Tbsp oil

1 Tbsp paprika

1 Tbsp pepper or 1 jalapeño pepper, chopped (remove seeds for less heat)

6 bay leaves

2 cubes chicken bouillon

salt

4 skinless chicken breasts, quartered (or the equivalent in any chicken parts)

water, enough to just cover chicken and vegetables

SPICED CHICKPEAS WITH CHICKEN

Serves 4 to 6

4 Tbsp oil

2 medium onions, finely chopped

1 head garlic, chopped

2 stalks celery, chopped (leaves included)

1 large tomato, chopped

1 green or red pepper, sliced

1 bunch parsley, chopped

½ medium whole chicken, skinned and quartered (or the equivalent in any chicken parts)

2 cans (19 oz/540 mL each) chickpeas, drained and rinsed, or 4 cups cooked dried chickpeas (see page 156)

5 cups water (or enough to cover ingredients)

1 can (5½ oz/156 mL) tomato paste

2 cubes chicken bouillon

seeds from 6 cardamom pods, crushed (optional)

2 Tbsp each allspice and cinnamon

1 Tbsp each pepper and nutmeg

½ Tbsp ground cloves

1 tsp turmeric

salt

lime wedges, for garnish (optional)

This quick, tasty dish goes a long way. It's also healthy and low in fat, and I love the aroma that fills the house when it's cooking. I serve it over white rice with a simple green salad on the side. When I have dinner parties, this is one of the dishes I am sure to make.

I met an Australian chap in university who was vibrant, progressive and well-liked by everyone. His dream was to complete his PhD and then work in Africa. He got involved with and subsequently married a woman who was in the same doctoral program but whom no one else could stand. Despite this, I invited him over with his partner from time to time.

One Christmas just after my husband and I moved to Toronto, this fellow asked if they could visit us. I left the key for them, as they were to arrive while I was at work. When I phoned to make sure everything was all right, his wife answered the phone. I told her I would be arriving late and asked if she would start dinner by taking the chicken out of the freezer, putting it in a big pot filled with water and a little salt and leaving it on the stove over low heat. I told her to phone me if she had any questions. She didn't, so I phoned a couple of times to check in, and she said everything was going well.

A few hours later I came home to smell gas and see her sitting comfortably in the living room, reading a book. I ran to the kitchen and noticed that, yes, she had turned on the gas, but the element had not lit. All the windows were closed, and the odour of gas was unbearable. I am surprised the house had not exploded. I turned off the gas and ran around opening every window in the house.

When I had calmed down, I went back to the kitchen to cook. I noticed that she had put the chicken in the pot but had not bothered to remove its wrapping. At that point I was too tired to get mad; I just started to laugh and proceeded to cook the chicken and chickpeas dish I had planned. You can only imagine what the conversation around the table was about.

1. In a pot, warm the oil over low heat. Add the onions and garlic and sauté until light golden.
2. Stir in the celery, tomato, green or red pepper and parsley. Sauté for a few minutes.
3. Increase the heat to medium. Add the chicken and sauté for 5 to 7 minutes.
4. Add the remaining ingredients, stirring to mix well.
5. Bring the mixture to a boil, then reduce the heat and simmer, for 50 to 60 minutes, partially covered. Halfway through cooking, adjust spices to taste, adding more water if needed. You should be able to taste the allspice, cinnamon and black pepper.
6. Serve with lime wedges to squeeze over top, if you like.

YELLOW SPLIT PEA STEW WITH CHICKEN AND LIME

From the age of seven until the age of fifteen, I went on Saturdays for a sleepover at my Auntie Gourji's. She was a very sick woman with severe asthma. Auntie Gourji had six daughters; her only son died tragically at a young age. I remember my aunt as being a very sad woman, but without a single mean bone in her body.

She lived with her husband and daughters in a one-bedroom apartment. While my cousins sat around listening to the radio, my aunt would be in the kitchen juggling what little food she had to make dinner for eight or more people. It was not easy. The kitchen consisted of a tiny table, a little chair, and a tiny counter with a little gas cooker like the kind used for camping. Auntie Gourji often made yellow split pea stew with a few chicken necks, and it tasted great. She worried that she did not have enough for the girls, so she herself never ate until everyone else had eaten. With a smile, she would ask me if I wanted seconds, and she never once complained that she had to feed an extra person. I would say to her, "Auntie, I can go home to eat." But she would smile, hug me and say, "Look how happy my daughters are to be with you; stay with us."

1. In a deep pot, heat the oil over low heat. Add the onion and sauté until light golden.
2. Add the tomatoes and parsley. Simmer for 3 to 4 minutes.
3. Add the chicken. Increase the heat to medium and cook, stirring constantly, for 7 to 10 minutes, until the chicken is partially cooked.
4. Stir in the split peas and the remaining ingredients, including the saffron with its soaking water.
5. Increase the heat to medium-high and bring the mixture to a boil. Reduce the heat and simmer for at least 2 hours, partially covered, until the split peas and chicken are extremely tender. Taste occasionally and adjust seasonings, including the lime juice. Add more water as needed. The stew should have a slight lemony, peppery flavour.
6. Before serving, remove the chicken from the pot, cut into smaller pieces, removing the bones (watch out for the tiny ones). Return the chicken to the pot, stir, then serve with bread.

VARIATION

Instead of fresh lime juice, use the seeds from 8 to 10 cardamom pods, crushed.

Serves 4 to 6

4 Tbsp oil

1 large onion, finely chopped

2 large ripe tomatoes, chopped

1 bunch parsley, chopped

2 skinless chicken breasts (or the equivalent in any chicken parts), cut into chunks

1½ cups dried yellow split peas, soaked in cold water overnight, then drained

1 can (5½ oz/156 mL) tomato paste or 1 can (14 oz/398 mL) tomato sauce

¼ cup fresh lime juice

2 cubes chicken bouillon

1 Tbsp pepper

2 tsp turmeric

⅛ tsp saffron, steeped in 2 Tbsp hot water

salt

water, enough to generously cover ingredients

Auntie Gourji and her fiancé, Moshe, Baghdad, *c.* 1930

POTATO STEW WITH CHICKEN, TOMATO AND CARDAMOM

4 Tbsp oil

1 onion, finely chopped

1 head garlic, chopped

2 ripe tomatoes, chopped

1 bunch parsley, chopped

½ medium whole chicken, cut into pieces (or any chicken parts)

5 potatoes, quartered

1 lb green peas, canned or frozen

1 can (5½ oz/156 mL) tomato paste or 1 can (14 oz/398 mL) tomato sauce

2 cubes chicken bouillon

seeds from 8 cardamom pods, crushed (optional)

1 Tbsp pepper or 1 jalapeño pepper, chopped (remove seeds for less heat)

1 tsp turmeric

salt

water, enough to generously cover ingredients

Potato stew with meat is a common Iraqi dish. When I was growing up, this stew was served over a mound of rice and eaten with flatbread—starch over starch eaten with starch!—but it sure tasted good. Turn the clock forward almost forty years and I am in China, in Nanjing and Yiwu County, doing a documentary on the Japanese occupation of China during the Second World War. One of the volunteers who helped locate survivors was married to a Muslim Chinese woman and together they ran the local restaurant. For days before eating there, I had been hearing about the "Muslim food." A strange phrase, I thought—there are over one billion Muslims in the world, of many different cultures and on all continents. So what was meant by a "Muslim" dish? I went to the restaurant to find out. The food, I was sure, would be just a variation of Chinese food. I was wrong. Although some of the dishes were typical local Chinese recipes, others were very much a variation of Middle Eastern recipes. For example, the potato and chicken stew cooked in a tomato sauce was very much an Iraqi dish.

I was so excited to have familiar food that I announced to everyone in the restaurant that the potato stew was an Iraqi dish. As I was leaving, I turned to the owners and said *"Salam alekem"* (May peace be with you), an Arabic expression for saying goodbye. Very excited, they grasped my hands and touched my face. Perhaps they had never seen an Arab up close. I felt like I was a precious commodity.

As in the Middle East, in China this stew is served with rice, though a salad also goes well with it. The peas add sweetness.

1. In a pot, heat the oil over low heat. Sauté the onion and garlic until light golden.
2. Add the tomatoes and parsley, cover and cook for 2 to 3 minutes.
3. Increase the heat to medium and add the chicken. Sauté for 7 to 10 minutes, stirring constantly.
4. Add the remaining ingredients and increase the heat to medium-high.
5. Bring the mixture to a boil, then reduce the heat and simmer for 50 to 60 minutes, partially covered, until the chicken and potatoes are very tender. Halfway through cooking, taste the stew to make sure it has sufficient spices. If needed, add a little at a time, to taste. If more water is needed, add ½ cup at a time.

SWEET-AND-SOUR SQUASH WITH RAISINS AND MEATBALLS

This dish was one of my favourites when I was growing up. I ate it regularly. A few years ago, I ordered squash casserole at a university cafeteria. It was not very flavourful, but the memory it evoked is very dear to me.

My first year at university, I decided to start listening to classical music. During all my years in Europe, I had heard classical music in the homes where I worked. I hated it; it was painful to my ears. At the same time, I associated it with cultured people. So I forced myself to listen to it every day, at first for ten minutes, then gradually a few minutes more each day. I went from hating classical music to loving it. I was so proud of myself; I had conquered another hurdle.

A year later, young classical musicians from around the world gathered for two weeks to perform together at the university's conservatory. One day as I was eating my bowl of baked squash in the cafeteria, an elderly couple sat down next to me. Unbeknownst to me, they were the concerts' conductor and his wife. We started to talk, and very innocently I told them how I had taught myself to appreciate classical music. They were so moved by my story that they took the time to explain the various instruments, the sounds they make and how they come together in an orchestra. And they encouraged me to attend the final concert the youth were giving. Rachmaninoff, Brahms and Chopin, I believe it was.

It was the first classical concert I had ever attended, and I felt awkward. But once the music started, I was mesmerized by the magical sounds of the instruments. They took me to faraway places, and I was smiling and crying at the same time. I turned to the person sitting next to me and kissed her in my excitement.

I serve this dish over plain rice.

1. Cut the squash into quarters. Scoop out and discard the seeds. Place cut side up on a baking sheet lined with parchment paper. Sprinkle with cinnamon and olive oil and bake in a 400°F oven for 20 minutes. When partially cooked and soft enough to peel, remove from oven, peel and set aside.

2. Meanwhile, in a bowl, combine the meatball ingredients. Place next to the stove, along with a bowl of cold water.

3. In a large, deep pot, sauté the onions in the oil over low heat until light golden. Increase the heat to medium-low and add the tomato; sauté for 3 to 4 minutes.

4. Meanwhile, combine the sauce ingredients; set aside.

5. Using the palms of your hands moistened with cold water, shape the meat mixture into walnut-size balls. Sauté in the tomato mixture for a few minutes, then stir in the squash, raisins, carrots (if using), stew spices and sauce. Increase the heat to medium and bring to a boil, stirring to prevent sticking.

6. Reduce the heat and simmer for 60 minutes, partially covered. Halfway through, taste and make sure stew is not too sweet and not too sour, and has a touch of spiciness. If it needs more water, lemon juice, spices or sugar, add a little at a time, to taste.

Serves 6

Stew

2 squash of your choice (approx 2 lb each)

cinnamon, for sprinkling

olive oil, for sprinkling

2 onions, chopped

4 Tbsp oil

1 large tomato, chopped

1 cup raisins

2 large carrots, cut into rounds (optional)

2 Tbsp each cinnamon and allspice

1 Tbsp each nutmeg, pepper and sugar

1 tsp each ground cloves and turmeric

salt

Meatballs

1½ lb ground beef, chicken or turkey

1 onion, finely chopped

1 bunch parsley, finely chopped

1 egg

5 Tbsp water, plus extra as needed

4 Tbsp dried bread crumbs

1½ Tbsp each cinnamon and allspice

½ Tbsp pepper

2 tsp nutmeg

1 tsp each turmeric and ground cloves

salt

Sauce

5 cups water (or enough to cover ingredients)

2 cubes chicken bouillon

juice of 2 lemons

1 can (14 oz/398 mL) tomato sauce

3 Tbsp ketchup (optional)

ZUCCHINI STEW WITH TOMATO AND CORIANDER

Serves 4 to 6

1 large onion, chopped

1 head garlic, chopped

3 Tbsp oil

2 tomatoes, chopped

1 green pepper, sliced (optional)

2 lb stewing beef or ½ medium whole chicken, skinned and cut into pieces

5 medium zucchini, cut into rounds of medium thickness

1 bunch coriander or parsley, chopped

4 cups water (or enough to just cover ingredients)

Sauce

1 can (5½ oz/156 mL) tomato paste or 1 can (14 oz/398 mL) tomato sauce

juice 1 lemon or lime

2 cubes chicken bouillon

1 Tbsp brown sugar (optional)

2 tsp pepper

1 tsp turmeric

salt

Recently I went to the Middle East to visit family and friends. My mother, brothers, nephews and their families all live in what I think of as the Sharabani compound, a building with five floors and eleven apartments, all occupied by a Sharabani. My older brother, David, his three kids and my other brother work together. And David, his wife, his children and their families all go on vacation together. For a person living in North America, where personal space and privacy are crucial, this arrangement may sound overwhelming. But now that I have children and am older, I love the way of life in the Sharabani compound.

The week I was visiting, David had a special dinner to celebrate his daughter's wedding. Everyone in the building was involved in the preparation. Pots were carried up and down the stairs, and a different dish was cooking in each apartment on each floor. I was stationed upstairs, preparing, among other things, a zucchini stew. There was a lot of shouting—"Too much spice!" "Not enough spice!"—each cook knowing better than the other how to cook. It was all part of the experience. At one point my mother, Najiba, yelled at her sister, "You cook just like a Polish woman!" We all started laughing and couldn't stop. I have no idea what she meant by that. I looked around me and thought, their lives are so rich because they are surrounded by their families. My mother might say that my zucchini stew tastes like a Pole cooked it—well, it sure is tasty. I serve this dish with white rice.

NOTE: If making the meatball variation below, begin by preparing the meatball mixture, so that it is ready to add to the tomato mixture in Step 3.

1. In a large, deep pot over low heat, sauté the onion and garlic in the oil until light golden.
2. Add the tomatoes and green pepper (if using) and simmer for 4 minutes.
3. Increase the heat to medium and add the meat; sauté for 5 minutes. (Or, if preparing the meatball variation below, add the meatballs at this point.)
4. Meanwhile, in a small bowl, combine the sauce ingredients; set aside.
5. Add the zucchini, coriander, water (increase to 5 cups if making meatballs) and sauce to the onion-tomato mixture. The liquids should cover the vegetables and meat. Bring the mixture to a boil, then loosely cover. Reduce the heat and simmer for 45 to 60 minutes, partially covered, or until the meat and vegetables are very tender. Stir often to prevent sticking on the bottom.
6. When the meat is cooked through, taste the sauce; it should have a hint of lemon and a distinct coriander flavour. Adjust seasonings, a little at a time, to taste.

Instead of using stewing beef or chicken pieces, make beef or poultry meatballs. Follow the directions in the recipe, except use the sauce ingredients listed below, as the spices are slightly different.

1. *To prepare the meatballs,* in a large bowl, using your hands constantly moistened with cold water, combine the meatball ingredients.

2. Set the meatball mixture and a bowl with cold water next to the stove. Using the palms of your hands moistened with cold water, shape the meatball mixture into balls the size of walnuts; drop into the onion-tomato mixture as each is formed.

3. Once all the meatballs have been added to the onion-tomato mixture, increase the heat to medium-low and simmer until the meatballs are partially cooked, about 7 minutes. Continue as directed (Steps 4 to 6).

Serves 4 to 6

Meatballs

2 lb ground beef, chicken or turkey

1 onion, chopped

1 bunch parsley, chopped

1 egg

5 to 6 Tbsp cold water

4 Tbsp dried bread crumbs

1 Tbsp each allspice, cinnamon and pepper

1 tsp each nutmeg and ground cloves

salt

Sauce

½ can (5½ oz/156 mL) tomato paste or 1 can (14 oz/398 mL) tomato sauce

juice of 2 lemons or limes

2 cubes chicken or vegetable bouillon

1½ Tbsp pepper

1 Tbsp brown sugar (optional)

1 tsp turmeric

salt

SWEET-AND-SOUR EGGPLANT AND MEAT STEW

ENGRYAH

Serves 4 to 6

2 medium eggplants

4 Tbsp oil

1 large onion, sliced

1 head garlic, chopped

2 large ripe tomatoes, thinly
   sliced

2 stalks celery (leaves included)

1 red or green pepper, sliced

1 bunch parsley, chopped

2 lb stewing beef or boneless
   chicken (with or without
   skin), cut into chunks

Sauce

½ can (5½ oz/156 mL) tomato
   paste or 1 can (14 oz/398 mL)
   tomato sauce

juice of 2 lemons

2 cubes chicken or vegetable
   bouillon

2 Tbsp sugar

2 Tbsp ketchup (optional)

2 tsp pepper, or less to taste

1 tsp turmeric

salt

4 cups water, plus more
   as needed

In early 1960s, when I was only ten years old, Najiba, my mother, decided it was time for her brother, Abdallah, who lived in Iran, to get married. The key was to find him the right woman. With the help of her friends, my mother found Clara, who lived in Israel and came from a "good family." Above all, however, although she was Iraqi, Clara had a light complexion, considered an important quality in a woman. The joke used to be that it did not matter how many heads, arms or legs a woman had, so long as her complexion was light. The dowry was negotiated with Clara's parents and my uncle agreed to marry her, even though they had never met.

The engagement day came along, but Abdallah was nowhere to be seen. According to tradition, the engagement had to be blessed by a religious authority, and the ceremony went on as scheduled, without my uncle. Clara, the poor woman, was engaged to a picture. Yes, to a picture! A photograph of Abdallah was placed on the table, and guests congratulated Clara and blessed the picture. Later, the guests danced and sang around the picture. Of course, we had a table full of food, and one of the dishes was this eggplant stew, *engryah*. (And yes, Abdallah did make it to the wedding.)

I love this stew. I serve it over white rice, with a salad. It also freezes well.

1. Rinse and cut the eggplants into 1-inch-thick rounds. Bake or fry the eggplant (see page 55).

2. Meanwhile, heat the oil in a deep pot over low heat. Sauté the onion and garlic until light golden.

3. Add the tomatoes, celery, pepper and parsley and stir for 2 to 3 minutes, then cover.

4. Increase the heat to medium and add the meat. Sauté for 5 to 7 minutes, stirring occasionally to prevent sticking or burning.

5. Meanwhile, in a bowl, combine the sauce ingredients.

6. Gently spoon the cooked eggplant over the meat, then pour in the sauce. Add up to another 1 cup of water, so that the liquid just covers the vegetables and meat. Reduce the heat to medium-low. With a wooden spoon, gently stir the juices, jiggling the eggplant, until the liquid comes to a boil.

7. Reduce the heat and simmer for 45 to 60 minutes, partially covered. Every 20 minutes or so taste and adjust seasonings as desired, stirring them in gently. The stew should have a hint of lemon, with a touch of sweetness.

CURRIED GREEN BEANS AND BEEF WITH POTATOES AND HERBS

I lived in Berkeley years ago. I had saved up so that I could take the summer off work in Montreal to go to sunny California, and Hollywood. My first stop was Los Angeles.

While I was working as a chambermaid in London, I became friendly with a couple from LA who were staying at the hotel. When I told them that I dreamed of seeing California, they said that if I ever made it to LA, I should visit them.

I arrived in LA late at night and phoned the couple from the airport. They did not remember me but politely invited me to their home. But once I was there, it was clear that I wasn't wanted. It was they who suggested I go to Berkeley. I was naive and didn't know much about the place, or the hippie movement, but I took their advice. On the bus there I met two Iranians, students at the University of California. They found me a cheap rooming house close to the campus. I loved the city from the start. No one seemed to care what you did or who you were, so I hung around all sorts of people. I was taken to anti–Vietnam War demonstrations and to a concert with Joan Baez and Jimmy Hendricks.

But the best experience of all occurred one day as I was walking down the street. Ahead of me was a woman carrying groceries, accompanied by two little girls. She tripped and her groceries spilled onto the sidewalk. Naturally, I helped her pick them up and carry them home. Grateful, she insisted that I stay for a cup of tea. We started talking and, before I knew it, her husband arrived home from work. They both insisted that I stay for supper. For the next two weeks I was a regular at their house. And one day, Ljuba and her husband, Leon, insisted that I move in and stay the rest of the summer.

It was one of the warmest homes I've ever visited, open to all, like a central train station where everyone and anyone who passed by stopped and had a meal. On Friday at least a dozen people came for the beautiful dinner Ljuba prepared.

Ljuba became the sister I'd always wanted. We eventually lost touch, but our friendship was rekindled fifteen years later when my daughter went to Berkeley to study music. I still remember the first meal Ljuba served me, a bean dish with meat—though it did not really matter what she served; what I will always remember is the warmth and love. This dish stands on its own—it really doesn't even need rice or salad. Or omit the potatoes and serve with rice.

1. In a deep pot over low heat, sauté the onion and garlic in the oil until light golden.
2. Add the tomato and simmer for 2 to 3 minutes.
3. Add the meat, increase the heat to medium and cook for 5 to 7 minutes, stirring to prevent burning or lumps from forming. When the meat is almost cooked, add the remaining ingredients, stirring to mix well.
4. Bring the stew to a boil, then reduce the heat and simmer for 45 to 60 minutes, partially covered, or until the vegetables are tender. Stir frequently to prevent burning. Adjust seasonings to taste and add a little water to thin, if necessary.

Serves 4 to 6

1 large onion, chopped

1 head garlic, chopped

3 Tbsp oil

1 large tomato, chopped

2 lb ground beef, chicken or turkey

4 cups water

1½ lb green beans, frozen or fresh (trimmed)

2 medium potatoes, finely chopped

2 celery stalks, chopped

1 bunch parsley chopped

2 cubes chicken bouillon

2 Tbsp cumin

2 Tbsp curry powder

½ Tbsp turmeric

2 tsp pepper or chopped jalapeño pepper (remove seeds for less heat)

salt

BEEF AND SPINACH STEW WITH BEANS, LEMON AND HERBS

QORMEH SABZI

Serves 6 to 8

2 bunches each parsley, coriander and green onions, chopped, plus more to taste

3 pkgs (10 oz/284 g each) fresh spinach

2 large onions, chopped

4 Tbsp oil

2 lb stewing beef

2 cans (19 oz/540 mL each) red kidney beans and/or black-eyed peas, drained and rinsed, or 4 cups cooked dried beans and/or peas (see page 156)

2 cubes chicken bouillon

2 dried limes (seeds removed), crushed (optional)

2 tsp pepper

1 tsp turmeric

salt

juice of 4 lemons

3 cups boiling water

This is one of my favourite winter dishes. It fills the house with the beautiful fragrance of herbs and lemon. When I was growing up, I ate this dish at our dear neighbour Nasrat's. She would call across the balcony for me and my brothers, and within seconds we would be at her home, ready to eat.

I used to think that Nasrat was my own special Mother Angel. Years later I learned from my older brother that she shared her love not only with me but with many other children, especially needy ones. One of these children moved to Los Angeles and to express his gratitude invited Nasrat to visit him and his family there. My brother gave her my phone number in case Nasrat wanted to phone me from LA. And she did. In the middle of the night my phone rang.

"Hello, sweetie, it is me, Nasrat."

"Where are you?" I asked.

"I am in America, and I am coming to see you."

I tried to get more information from her, but to no avail. Four days later I received another phone call. "Hello? Is this Souad? I have a woman here at the bus terminal, her name is Nasrat and she wants to know how to get to your house." Nasrat could not read or write in any language, so upon arriving by bus in Toronto, alone, she could not read my phone number. A kind Lebanese man helped her, bringing her to my house.

She stayed with us for a couple of weeks. Even though she did not speak English, everyone who met her loved her. What is not to love about this woman who is all heart? I will never forget her sitting on my kitchen floor in Toronto, picking through bunches and bunches of herbs and greens spread all over the floor.

It is now a tradition in my house to make this dish in late fall or winter. I make it on a Sunday, when I have more time to prepare it. I serve it with either Saffron Rice (page 76) or Green Rice (page 77). I make enough to give to friends and neighbours, and freeze at least one extra meal's worth. You can also use chunks of chicken or turkey breast, though I prefer to use stewing beef. Dried limes are available in Middle Eastern food stores.

◈ ◈ ◈

Nasrat, Toronto, 1986

1. Rinse the parsley, coriander, green onions and spinach well in cold water. Drain and chop coarsely. In a bowl, combine the chopped greens; set aside.
2. In a large, deep pot, sauté the onions in the oil over low heat until light golden.
3. Increase the heat to medium-low and add the meat. Sauté until the meat is almost cooked through.
4. Gradually add the greens, covering the pot with each batch until the greens wilt.
5. Stir in the beans, bouillon cubes, dried limes (if using) and spices. Add the juice of 2 lemons (half the total amount called for); let the mixture cook for a few minutes, then add more lemon juice to taste.
6. Add 2 cups of the water, gradually adding more throughout cooking time if needed.
7. Reduce the heat and simmer for 45 to 60 minutes, partially covered, until the meat and vegetables are extremely soft. Gradually add any remaining lemon juice to taste as the stew cooks. The stew should not be too lemony; if it is, add more greens.

SPINACH AND GROUND BEEF WITH PINE NUTS AND LEMON

Serves 4 to 6

1 large onion, chopped

1 head garlic, chopped

4 Tbsp oil

2 lb ground beef

3 pkgs (10 oz/284 g each) fresh
   spinach

juice of 2 lemons

2 cubes chicken bouillon

1 tsp pepper

salt

1 cup water

½ cup pine nuts

This typical Lebanese and Palestinian dish has a delicate flavour that grows easily on you and is simple to make. I serve this dish with white rice. You can use ground chicken or turkey instead of beef if you like. You could also use Swiss chard or kale instead of spinach—but only 1 or 2 bunches.

◈   ◈   ◈

1. In a large, deep pot over low heat, sauté the onion and garlic in the oil until golden.
2. Add the meat, increase the heat to medium-low, and cook, stirring constantly, until the meat is cooked.
3. Add the spinach, one package at a time, allowing each batch to wilt before adding the next.
4. Add the lemon juice, bouillon cubes, pepper, salt and water. Stir for a few minutes to mix well, then cover and simmer for 20 minutes, until the meat is cooked through. Adjust lemon juice and spices to taste.
5. Meanwhile, toast the pine nuts on a baking sheet for 3 to 4 minutes in a 350°F oven or in a heavy frying pan on the stovetop until light golden. Watch carefully, as they burn quickly.
6. When the meat is cooked, remove the stew from the heat and stir in the pine nuts.

GARLIC STEW WITH BEEF, MINT AND LEMON
THOUMIYA

Most people think of garlic as a base ingredient in stews rather than as the primary ingredient. But in the Middle East, garlic is used in generous quantities, and there are several garlic dishes, both as main courses and as sides.

I loved this stew as a child, and I love it now. My son loves it too, and always requests it for his birthday dinner.

This is a delicate dish, although it is rather a lot of work to peel all the garlic, and your hands will smell of it afterward (rinsing them with lemon juice will help). Some grocery stores sell bags of peeled garlic; it costs more but will save you a lot of time. I sometimes use lamb or skinless chicken breast for this dish, but I prefer the stewing beef. I serve the stew over white rice, with a salad on the side.

1. Warm the oil in a pot over very low heat. Add the onions and garlic and cook until light golden.
2. Add the tomatoes, parsley, green onions and peppers. Cover for 3 to 4 minutes, until the juices come out.
3. Add the meat, increase the heat slightly and sauté, stirring, until the meat is lightly browned.
4. Stir in the remaining ingredients. Bring the mixture to a boil, then reduce the heat and simmer for 1½ to 2 hours, partially covered. After about 20 minutes of cooking, taste and adjust seasonings; the stew should taste of lemon, with a touch of sweetness, garlic and mint. (Keep in mind that it takes a while for the flavours to come out—the longer the stew cooks, the more the sweetness of the garlic comes out.) If adding more garlic or onion, sauté first with a little oil in a separate pan.

Serves 6 to 8

5 Tbsp oil

2 medium or large onions, chopped

8 heads garlic, thinly sliced

2 large ripe tomatoes, finely chopped

1 bunch parsley, finely chopped

2 bunches green onions, finely chopped

1 each green and red pepper, chopped

2½ lb stewing beef or boneless, skinless chicken breast, cut into chunks

5 cups water (or enough to cover ingredients)

1 cup fresh lemon juice

6 bunches fresh mint, leaves picked and chopped

2 cubes chicken bouillon

1½ Tbsp sugar

2 tsp pepper

1 tsp turmeric

salt

When I was growing up, main-course meat or poultry dishes were cooked only for special occasions. Not only were red meat and poultry expensive, but I lived in a hot climate and my family, like many others, did not have a freezer or refrigerator in which to store the meat. Even these meat and chicken dishes—including kubbe (page 111), or shish kebabs (page 114)— use plenty of herbs and spices.

MEAT AND POULTRY

Spiced Meatballs

MARINATED STEAK

Serves 4 to 6

2½ to 3 lb steak
5 Tbsp soy sauce
½ tsp chili flakes
½ tsp paprika
½ tsp garlic powder
½ tsp cumin
½ tsp coriander seeds
½ tsp curry powder
¼ tsp turmeric

The first time I ate at my parents-in-law's house, I was shocked that the meal consisted of a tiny amount of salad, some corn and a huge steak each. Looking around the table, I saw how much everyone was enjoying their steaks. But for me, being served such a huge piece of meat was a completely unfamiliar experience.

After being with my husband for many years, I am getting used to eating steak from time to time. For years I was willing to go along, having a barbecued steak with absolutely nothing on it. But in the last few years I have been marinating the steak for a few hours before cooking it. And in the words of my husband, who has eaten steak all his life, "This is the best steak I have ever had." With a steak, I usually serve a simple salad and rice.

Less expensive cuts of meat work well for this recipe, as the marinade acts as a tenderizer. However, I find that the thicker the cut, the better it absorbs the marinade.

1. In a bowl, combine the soy sauce and spices.
2. Place the steak in a casserole dish. Using a fork, prick the steak on both sides. Drizzle half of the spice mixture on each side of the steak. Cover the dish and refrigerate for 2 to 4 hours.
3. Half an hour before barbecuing, remove the steak from the refrigerator and bring to room temperature. Barbecue on medium heat (350°F) for 8 to 10 minutes per side for medium-rare.

SPICED MEATBALLS
KUBBE

On hot summer days when I was growing up in Israel, my family, like many Iranian families, often went to a nearby park that had a pond. None of us had cars, so we went there by bus. A dozen of us, old and young, would carry our little Hibachi, food, drinks, a samovar and, of course, as good Iranians, a carpet. Pushing and shoving onto an already packed bus, we managed to get there. And the first thing we did was lay down our huge carpet, close to the other families.

Here in North America, we're always yearning for space and privacy—in enclosed backyards, isolated cottages and private beaches. In the Middle East, "privacy" and "tranquility" were not part of our vocabulary. Also not part of our vocabulary was small food portions. On this particular day, our neighbour Nasrat was getting the Hibachi ready, her daughter and other relatives were mixing the *kubbe,* someone set up a gas barbecue to put a huge pot of rice on, others were preparing the salads and slicing the watermelon, and Nasrat's husband prepared the samovar. For us as kids, it was heaven. All day and night, into the wee hours of the morning, we ate and played, sometimes snoozed, other times joined the adults to listen to their stories, singing and gossiping.

The closest I come now to that same feeling of community is in the summertime when I make *kubbe* and serve my family, neighbours and friends. They love it, and I love seeing them enjoy it. You can freeze any extras.

1. In a deep bowl, combine all the ingredients. Keep a bowl of cold water at hand to moisten your hands as you shape the meatballs. (If not using bread crumbs, the mixture will not shape firmly; just drop walnut-size portions onto the prepared baking sheet without attempting to make firm balls.)
2. Place the meatballs on a baking sheet lined with parchment paper and bake in a 425°F oven for 20 to 25 minutes.

VARIATION
Soak ½ cup fine bulgur in warm water for 30 minutes, drain, then gently squeeze a handful at a time to remove any excess water. Mix with the recipe ingredients (Step 1) and continue as directed.

Serves 6 to 8

2 lb ground beef, chicken or turkey

1 large onion, finely chopped

1 bunch parsley, finely chopped

1 egg

5 Tbsp cold water

4 Tbsp dried bread crumbs (optional)

2 Tbsp cumin

1½ Tbsp each allspice and cinnamon

1 Tbsp each ground cloves and pepper

2 tsp nutmeg

salt

BULGUR KUBBE WITH PINE NUTS AND RAISINS

KUBBE BULGUR BIS-SINIYAH

Serves 6 to 8

Filling

3 Tbsp oil

1 large onion, very thinly sliced

2 lb ground beef, chicken or turkey

1½ Tbsp each allspice, cinnamon and cumin

1 Tbsp pepper

1 tsp each ground cloves and turmeric

salt

1 bunch parsley, finely chopped

1 cup raisins

½ cup pine nuts

Shell

1 lb ground beef, chicken or turkey

1½ cups fine bulgur or cracked wheat, soaked in cold water for 30 to 60 minutes, then drained

1 large onion, quartered

5 Tbsp cold water

1 Tbsp each allspice and cinnamon

1 Tbsp pepper

salt

olive oil, for sprinkling

During a recent visit to Israel, I went to my brother's house in Ramat Gan. The house was full with cousins, nephews, aunts and other relatives, all sitting, talking, laughing and eating. A huge table was laden with appetizers, salads, fruits, nuts and desserts. We ate and talked late into the night, then the conversation turned to—what else—food. My aunt told us of the restaurant that served the best *kubbe bulgur* she had ever eaten, my cousin claimed she made the best *kubbe bulgur* and then my brother chimed in saying that he knew the restaurant that served the best and to prove it we should all go there that night.

So we drove in a convoy of three cars to the restaurant, despite having already eaten. We arrived to find the owner and his family closing up for the night. But he knew my brother, who just marched into the dark restaurant, turned on the light and pulled the chairs down off the tables. We had barely time to settle into our seats before our three tables were covered with platters of food. How would we ever be able to clear the table of all the dishes after what we had eaten at my brother's house? But the food was so scrumptious, it wasn't difficult.

This *kubbe* is one of my husband's favourite meals, though I don't make it often because it is rich and rather time-consuming to make. The *kubbe* can be made either as individual pieces or in a large pan like a lasagne that you then cut into squares. I often serve the *kubbe* with Green Salad with Lemon Garlic Dressing (page 26), pickles and tahini (page 14).

◇　◇　◇

1. *To prepare the filling,* in a frying pan, heat the oil over low heat. Fry the onion until light golden. Add the meat and spices, including the salt and pepper, mixing well.
2. Increase the heat to medium and cook until the meat is browned, adding the parsley, raisins and pine nuts 2 or 3 minutes before the meat is cooked. Remove the pan from the heat.
3. *To prepare the shell,* in a food processor, mix the ground meat, bulgur (squeezing out any excess water a handful at a time), onion, water and spices until combined. You may need to do this in 2 or 3 batches.
4. Line a 9- × 13-inch lasagne pan with parchment paper. Spoon half of the shell mixture into the pan. Moisten your hands with cold water, then firmly press the mixture to cover the bottom of the pan and a little up the sides.
5. Spread the filling on the shell.
6. Using your hands constantly moistened with cold water, flatten the remaining shell mixture a little at a time and place it on top of the filling. Repeat until the filling is completely covered, like patchwork. Finally, press the shell top together, sealing the edges.
7. Deeply score the *kubbe* diagonally or into squares. Sprinkle with olive oil. Bake in a 400°F oven for 60 to 80 minutes, until browned and crispy.

POTATO PATTIES WITH MEAT, RAISINS AND PINE NUTS

This was one of my favourite foods as a kid. It is a potato shell filled with ground beef or chicken, raisins and pine nuts.

Ever since I was young, my mother attended political rallies. She was never interested in politics, nor did she have any commitment or affiliation to any particular political party. But she loved the free bus rides around the country that were organized by the various parties. Of course, she had to then participate in the rallies. Inevitably, she would boo the candidate, call him names and make so much noise that people could not hear his speech. She absolutely loved doing this. And then she returned home with stories to tell. She went to rallies until she was in her mid-eighties. Apparently, at one of the more recent rallies, the organizers had enough of her and threw her off the bus, despite her kicking and screaming. Who can blame them?

I cannot imagine that many of you will follow her example, but you may try to make these potato patties—the dish she often packed for the rallies. Serve with a salad, pickles and olives. Garnish the serving platter with sprigs of parsley. Extras can be frozen (uncooked) in a flat container, layered between waxed paper.

1. *To prepare the filling,* in a frying pan over medium heat, heat the oil. Sauté the onion until light golden.
2. Add the meat and spices, increase the heat and sauté until the meat is cooked through.
3. Reduce the heat to simmer. Add the raisins and pine nuts. Sauté for 2 to 3 minutes. Remove from the heat, add the parsley and stir to mix well.
4. *To prepare the shell,* in a large pot filled with lightly salted water, boil the potatoes until very tender; drain.
5. Mash the potatoes with the egg and salt, until the mixture is smooth.
6. Divide the dough into egg-size portions. Spread the bread crumbs on a plate. Moisten your hands with cold water and flatten each ball between your palms.
7. Place a scant tablespoon of filling in the centre of a flattened shell, fold shell and pinch closed. Using the palms of your hands, roll into a ball and dredge in the bread crumbs. Place on a baking sheet lined with parchment paper and flatten with the back of a fork. Repeat until all the patties are assembled, then refrigerate for at least 1 hour before cooking.
8. Bring the patties to room temperature while the oven preheats to 375°F. Sprinkle the patties with olive oil and bake for 20 to 25 minutes or until browned.

VARIATION

In a frying pan, heat some oil for frying over high heat. Reduce the heat to medium-low and brown the patties on each side, being careful not to overcrowd in the pan. Drain on a plate lined with paper towel, if necessary layering between paper towel.

Serves 6 to 8

Filling

3 Tbsp oil

1 large onion, finely chopped

1½ lb lean ground beef, chicken or turkey

1½ Tbsp allspice

1 tsp turmeric

1 tsp pepper

salt

1 cup raisins

½ cup pine nuts

½ cup finely chopped parsley

Shell

2 lb potatoes, peeled, sliced into quarters

1 egg

salt

dried bread crumbs

olive oil, for sprinkling

LEMON-CHILI SHISH KEBABS

Serves 6

6 12-inch wooden skewers,
 soaked in water for 1 hour

2 lb chicken breasts or beef
 steak, cut into chunks

2 red, yellow or orange peppers,
 cut into chunks (optional)

1 large onion, cut into chunks
 (optional)

mushrooms

cherry tomatoes

Marinade

2 cups plain yogurt

¼ cup fresh lemon or lime juice

5 cloves garlic, crushed, with a
 pinch of salt

2 Tbsp olive oil

1 Tbsp Dijon mustard

1 Tbsp each cumin, dried thyme
 and dried oregano

½ Tbsp chili pepper

salt

Variation:
Soy Sauce and Chili Marinade

¼ cup soy sauce

2 Tbsp each dried oregano and
 cumin

1 Tbsp each curry powder,
 paprika and coriander seeds

½ Tbsp each chili flakes and
 turmeric

Since my university years, I have joined in many political demonstrations against occupations, apartheid and war. In a demonstration against the Israeli war in Lebanon, a friend and I were surrounded by people who vehemently opposed our stance and started to argue with us and insult us. At first I politely tried to explain my position, but when I heard the hate and insults coming my way, I yelled back and stepped on the foot of one of the demonstrators. The man stepped back with a yelp.

After the demonstration, my friend and I stopped for shish kebab, and talked and laughed about the incident. But I had to soon leave for an interview for a documentary.

I arrived at my meeting place a few minutes early, set up my tape machine and looked over my questions. The door opened and who do I see but the man whose foot I had stepped on. Staring at me, he asked, "Don't I know you from somewhere?"

"No, of course not," I said. My legs were shaking, and I told myself to stay calm. I kept the interview as short as I could, but he kept eyeing me and saying, "I could swear I saw you somewhere …" And I would reply, "I have a very common face …"

For shish kebab I often buy both chicken and beef and ask the butcher to chop it into chunks. Because the beef is tenderized by the marinade, you don't need to buy the best cuts. I serve the shish kebabs on white rice or in a pita, with green salad on the side.

1. In a bowl, combine the marinade ingredients.
2. Add the meat and vegetables, toss to coat and let marinate in the refrigerator for at least 3 hours.
3. Thread the meat and vegetables alternately onto the skewers, leaving a tiny space between each piece.
4. Bake on a baking sheet lined with parchment paper in a 425°F oven for 6 to 8 minutes per side. Or barbecue over medium-high heat for 6 to 8 minutes per side.

VARIATION: SOY SAUCE AND CHILI MARINADE

In a bowl, combine the marinade ingredients. Add the meat and vegetables, toss to coat and let marinate in the refrigerator for at least 3 hours. Continue as directed (Step 3).

POMEGRANATE CHICKEN

Serves 6

The day we moved my daughter, Anna, into her university residence was a very sad day for all of us. On the way home, I decided to do some food shopping. I wanted to make one of Anna's favourite meals for dinner. As I picked up the items, I started to cry and could not stop. There I was, standing in line to pay, still crying. The young cashier stared at me while I explained through my tears that my daughter had left for university.

Iranians typically make pomegranate chicken for special occasions. It is very sweet and rich. If you prefer a less-rich dish, omit the walnuts. Serve on a bed of white rice.

1. Heat the oil in a pan over low heat. Add the onions and sauté until light golden.
2. Increase the heat to medium-low, add the walnuts (if using) and sauté for 2 to 3 minutes.
3. Add the chicken; sauté for 5 to 7 minutes. When the chicken is partially cooked, add the remaining ingredients, including the saffron with its soaking water. The liquid should cover the chicken; if it doesn't, add more water, orange juice and pomegranate molasses or juice.
4. Increase the heat to medium-high and bring the mixture to a boil. Reduce the heat and simmer for 1 hour or until the meat is falling off the bone. Stir the chicken occasionally, tasting after 20 minutes of cooking and adjusting ingredients to taste, a little at a time. The flavour should be of the sweet pomegranate. If it is too sweet, add a little fresh lemon juice; if too thick, add water.

4 Tbsp oil or butter

2 large onions, chopped

2 cups chopped walnuts (optional)

1 medium whole chicken, skinned and cut into 8 pieces (or the equivalent in any chicken parts)

6 Tbsp pomegranate molasses plus 5 cups combination of water and orange juice, or 3 cups pomegranate juice plus 2 cups combination of water and orange juice

3 Tbsp grated orange peel

2 cubes chicken bouillon

2 Tbsp sugar

1 Tbsp cinnamon

1½ tsp turmeric

⅛ tsp saffron threads, steeped in 2 Tbsp hot water

salt and pepper

BARBECUED LEMON-CHILI CHICKEN

Serves 4 to 6

1 medium whole chicken,
    skinned and cut into 8 to
    10 pieces (or the equivalent
    in any chicken parts)

¼ cup soy sauce

¼ cup lemon juice

2 Tbsp garlic powder

½ Tbsp chili flakes

This chicken dish reminds me of an experience I had in a market near Lake Malawi, where I had joined a group of Canadian students in Africa to do some volunteer work. One day we visited Father Boucher at the Ku Ngoni Centre of Culture and Art, near the village of Mua in the Mtakataka district. Father Boucher was a leading expert in the role of masks in traditional Malawian society. Academics and historians came from all over the world to study with him.

He was more than happy to give us a tour of the place and tell us about his work and the role of masks in traditional Malawian society. Afterward, we walked to the nearby market and found a tiny family-run restaurant. It had a minuscule kitchen with a couple of burners, and a single table with a couple of chairs. The owner had never had so many customers at one time, but he welcomed us with open arms. Within minutes, he had managed to gather his extended family to help prepare and serve a meal. We sat every which way, indoors and outdoors, while the roosters ran about our feet and the local kids played with us. Finally, the food was served—barbecued chicken and rice.

I serve this dish with rice on the side. You can also add a little bit of pickle, hot pepper or tahini (page 14) on the side, which will give the meal a whole new flavour.

◈   ◈   ◈

1. Place the chicken in a baking dish.
2. In a small bowl, combine the remaining ingredients. Pour over the chicken and refrigerate for at least 1 hour (the longer the chicken marinates, the more tender and tasty it will be).
3. Remove the chicken from the refrigerator. Spoon up any marinade from the bottom of the dish and drizzle over the chicken. Bake in a 425°F oven for 45 minutes, basting occasionally (or barbecue over medium heat for 20 minutes each side), until the juices run clear.

VARIATION

Omit the soy sauce and instead add 1 cup plain yogurt, 2 Tbsp cumin and 1 Tbsp dried thyme or dried basil.

CHICKEN BAKED WITH FRESH HERBS

One of my childhood memories of Iran is of our neighbours coming into the common courtyard at night, rolling out a carpet and setting dishes of food in the centre for people to sit around and eat from. Among the dishes there were always at least two types of rice—maybe sweet rice and green rice—and a couple of poultry dishes made with herbs. Of course, no one ate on the run but, rather, stayed to talk late into the night.

Herbs are a big part of Iranian cuisine—the more the merrier. Typically, we add herbs when cooking, but here the chicken is marinated first with herbs for extra flavour. For this recipe, you are better off using a little more lemon rather than less. I serve this dish with Green Rice (page 77) or plain white rice and a salad with vinaigrette dressing.

1. In a large bowl, combine the marinade ingredients.
2. Add the poultry and stir to coat. Refrigerate, covered, for at least 8 hours or overnight.
3. Barbecue the chicken over medium heat for 20 minutes per side. Or transfer to an ovenproof dish, drizzle the marinade over top, and bake in a 425°F oven for 45 to 60 minutes, basting occasionally, until the juices run clear.

VARIATION

If using turkey breast, flatten the breast and place half of the marinade in the centre. Fold the breast closed and tie with kitchen string. Top with the remaining marinade. Place in a resealable bag in a bowl and refrigerate for 8 hours or overnight. Barbecue on medium heat for about 25 to 35 minutes per side, or bake with the marinade, basting occasionally, in a 425°F oven for about 50 to 60 minutes, until the juices run clear.

Serves 6

4 skinless chicken breasts or 1 large skinless turkey breast, quartered (or the equivalent in any chicken or turkey parts)

Marinade

8 cloves garlic, chopped, with a pinch of salt

1 large onion, chopped

1 bunch green onions, chopped

½ bunch each coriander, parsley and dill, finely chopped

juice of 3 lemons

2 cubes chicken bouillon

2 Tbsp Dijon mustard

1 Tbsp pepper or 1 jalapeño pepper, chopped (remove seeds for less heat)

salt

IRAQI CHICKEN WITH RICE
TABYEET

Serves 6 to 8

3 to 4 lb whole chicken

Stuffing

1 onion, chopped

2 Tbsp oil

1 tomato, chopped

½ cup chopped parsley

1 cup chicken broth

½ cup boiling water

¼ cup long-grain white rice,
soaked in cold water for
1 hour, then drained

½ cup each raisins and pine nuts
(optional)

½ tsp each salt, pepper,
turmeric, ground cardamom,
allspice, cinnamon, ground
cloves and nutmeg

Rice

4 Tbsp oil

1 large onion, chopped

2 ripe tomatoes, chopped

1 bunch parsley, chopped

3 cups boiling water

1 can (5½ oz/156 mL) tomato
paste

2 cubes chicken bouillon

1½ Tbsp each allspice and
cinnamon

1 Tbsp cardamom pods, shelled
and seeds crushed

1 Tbsp pepper

2 tsp nutmeg

1 tsp each ground cloves and
turmeric

salt

2 cups long-grain white rice,
soaked in cold water for
1 hour, then drained

This Iraqi-Jewish dish is typically served for lunch on Saturday, the Sabbath. It is prepared Friday morning and left to cook very slowly overnight. In the morning, the chicken is crispy, the rice nicely dry with a crust (my favourite part) and the house filled with a tantalizing aroma. By noon, the chicken and rice have been arranged on a serving platter with salad and pita bread. Relatives, neighbours and friends drop by on Saturdays, and they know to help themselves to the *tabyeet*.

This version doesn't require overnight cooking. The chicken could also be made with the stuffing.

1. *To prepare the chicken and stuffing,* rinse the chicken and pat dry with paper towel.

2. In a large frying pan over very low heat, sauté the onion in the oil until light golden. Add the tomato and parsley and cook for 3 to 4 minutes.

3. Add the remaining stuffing ingredients, stirring to mix well. Increase the heat slightly and cook for 15 to 20 minutes. Remove the mixture from the heat and let cool slightly, then stuff the chicken, tying the chicken legs together with kitchen string.

4. *To prepare the rice,* in a large, deep, heavy-bottomed ovenproof dish, heat 2 Tbsp of the oil over very low heat. Add the onion and sauté until light golden.

5. Add the tomatoes and parsley; simmer for 3 to 4 minutes. Increase the heat to medium and place the stuffed chicken in the pot. Brown on all sides.

6. Add the remaining rice ingredients except for the reserved 2 Tbsp oil and the rice itself. Cover the pot loosely, bring the mixture to a boil, then reduce the heat to low.

7. After about 30 minutes, taste the broth and adjust the spices to taste. If the broth seems too thick, add a little more water. Continue to cook for another 25 minutes, then transfer the chicken to a serving platter.

8. Add the rice to the broth, and more spices if desired (the broth should have a strong flavour and the liquids should just cover the rice). Bring to a boil, then reduce the heat to low.

9. When the water is almost all absorbed, return the chicken to the pot, placing it in the centre and pushing the rice to the sides so that the chicken touches the bottom of the pot. Drizzle the remaining 2 Tbsp oil over the chicken and rice. Cover the pot tightly and simmer over low heat for about 2 hours, until the rice forms a golden crust on the bottom and the chicken is almost falling off the bone.

10. Sprinkle the rice with cold water. To loosen the crust on the bottom, place the pot in cold water in the sink (the water should not be much past the bottom of the pot) for 5 minutes.

11. Remove the chicken and place on a large serving platter. Remove the stuffing and transfer to a serving bowl. Arrange the rice around the chicken.

Once the rice is cooked and the chicken has been returned to the pot, bake, uncovered, in a 400°F oven for 45 minutes, until a leg moves freely in its socket. Reduce the temperature to 325°F and cook for 2 hours.

Just before serving, sprinkle the rice with cold water. To loosen the crust on the bottom, place the pot in cold water in the sink (the water should not be much past the bottom of the pot) for 5 minutes. Remove the chicken and place on a large serving platter. Remove the stuffing and transfer to a bowl. Arrange the rice around the chicken.

CARDAMOM CHICKEN AND CHICKPEA BALLS

This is a typical Iranian dish that Nasrat, our neighbour in Israel, made frequently.

Nasrat used to tell me, "This dish is the poor man's dish." My brothers and I loved it. Whenever we smelled it cooking, we'd rush over to her house and beg for some. Of course, Nasrat, like most of us, made enough for her family and more.

In those days we used a cast-iron *hawan*, or pestle and mortar, to hammer the chicken breast and chickpeas until they were smooth, which could take hours. Today, I use a pestle and mortar to crush the garlic, I buy ground chickpeas at a Middle Eastern or Indian grocery store and I use the food processor for the rest. The cardamom is optional.

1. In a food processor, combine the chickpea ball ingredients until the mixture is smooth—do this in batches if necessary.
2. Transfer the mixture to a large bowl and, with your hands constantly moistened with cold water, shape the mixture into balls slightly larger than golf balls. Place on a baking sheet lined with waxed paper, then chill in the freezer for 1 hour.
3. Remove the chickpea balls from the freezer. In a large pot, combine the ingredients for the chicken broth, bring to a boil, and gently drop in the chickpea balls. Boil for a few minutes, reduce the heat and simmer for 30 to 45 minutes.
4. Serve hot, either in the broth or removed from the broth and accompanied with a salad.

Makes about 15 chickpea balls

Chickpea Balls

1 lb ground chicken or turkey

1 large onion, chopped

½ bunch parsley, chopped

2 cups chickpea flour

1 egg

5 Tbsp water, plus more as needed

½ Tbsp pepper

3 cloves garlic, minced, or 1 Tbsp garlic powder

1 tsp crushed cardamom seeds (shell pods) (optional)

1 tsp cumin

salt

Chicken Broth

7 to 9 cups water

1 large onion

2 cubes chicken bouillon

½ bunch parsley, chopped

seeds from 6 cardamom pods

1 tsp turmeric

salt and pepper

There are a few Iraqi and other Middle Eastern seafood recipes I remember from growing up, such as fried whitefish and Salauna ben Babanjan—Sweet-and-Sour Fish and Eggplant Casserole (page 131)—but most of the seafood recipes in this book are variations of dishes I ate or cooked in Latin America, Europe and Canada, where seafood is much more popular.

SEAFOOD

Sautéed Shrimp with Hot Chili Tomato Sauce

CEVICHE

Serves 4 to 6

1½ lb very fresh seafood (e.g.,
    a combination of whitefish,
    snapper, tuna and sea bass
    fillets and scallops)

1 red onion, finely sliced

1 red pepper, thinly sliced

1 stalk celery, finely chopped
    (leaves included)

1 bunch green onions, finely
    chopped

½ bunch each parsley and
    coriander, finely chopped

Marinade

6 cloves garlic, crushed with a
    pinch of salt, plus more to
    taste

1 jalapeño pepper with seeds,
    minced

juice of 5 limes

juice of 5 lemons

salt

You can find ceviche at just about any restaurant or market in Peru. It is raw white fish and shellfish marinated in lemon and lime juice, with assorted herbs. The acids in the citrus juices "cook" the fish.

In my early twenties I lived for a few months in Arequipa, a city in the Andes mountains, in southwestern Peru, having followed a friend who was teaching at the university there. One day, my friend noticed a sign on a storefront that read: "Come in and sign up for the annual climb of Monte Blanco." People came from all over to climb this mountain. It is not Mount Everest by any stretch of the imagination, but still …

My friend went in to inquire and ended up signing up for the climb. He persuaded me to do the same. I don't know what came over me. I do not do sports. My favourite pastime is going for coffee with a friend and talking. But I signed up, knowing I would never do the climb.

The next morning, journalists with cameras were standing outside my house. They told me they were looking for the woman who had signed up to climb Monte Blanco. When I said it was me, the cameras started rolling and I was bombarded with questions. I was too embarrassed to tell them I am hopeless at sports, so I made up stories about my skiing achievements. The next day, I opened the local newspaper and saw my picture with the headline "La Unica Mujer—The only woman who is going to climb this mountain is representing Canada." Apparently, a woman had climbed the mountain only once, fifty years earlier. That was not the end of it, though. Day after day, stories about me appeared in the newspaper. One claimed I represented Canada in a European ski competition (at that time, I had never even ever worn ski boots).

The night before the climb, city officials invited the participants for picture-taking and a dinner, where we were served ceviche and *chichi*—hard, roasted corn kernels. I was nibbling on the kernels, pondering how I could get out of the mess I had got myself into, when I felt wind whisk through my mouth, and then pain. I could feel that my two front crowns were missing. They had fallen out and I had swallowed them along with the kernels. Needless to say, my mouth was extremely sore and getting worse by the minute. But how would I possibly find a dentist so late at night? Fortunately, the participant sitting next to me noticed my distress and said he knew of a dentist, the only one in town. We rushed to the dentist's house, dragging him out of bed so that he could do the dental work.

The next afternoon, a military truck drove the climb participants to the foot of the mountain, in a village a few hours from Arequipa. We were to climb all night, reaching the peak at sunrise. Well-wishers, journalists and officials came to send us off. I was still in a state of shock, scared but unable to run away. As we started the climb, the guide warned us to stay in the centre of the mountain path, since the ground got icy and the path dropped away on both sides. At that point I said to myself, *That's it—I am not going to kill myself!* Petrified of both ice and heights, I turned around. With all the pushing and shoving going on, no one even noticed me leave. I asked some local kids if there was anywhere I could stay the night. One took me to his grandmother's home.

The house was a single room with no windows, with a llama inside and at least twelve people already asleep. They were sprawled every which way and I had to be careful not to step on anyone. At sunrise, as the women prepared breakfast before leaving for the fields, I told them the whole story in my broken Spanish. They laughed uncontrollably. The media were still in the village, and so the grandmother devised a plan: to wrap my legs with paper and cloth. "When you go out, just pretend you broke your leg," she said.

With fond memories of Peru and of the people I met across that beautiful land, I share with you a recipe for one of the dishes I ate there regularly—ceviche. I will not give you a recipe for roasted kernels, for obvious reasons. Serve the ceviche with bread or with boiled potatoes and a salad on the side. You can also serve it as a starter.

◈   ◈   ◈

1. Rinse the fish fillets and scallops and pat dry with paper towel. Cut into small chunks and place in a deep glass bowl (do not use plastic or metal).
2. Add the vegetables and herbs to the bowl.
3. In a separate bowl, combine the marinade ingredients. Pour over the fish and vegetables, stirring to mix well. Cover and refrigerate for 8 to 10 hours. The seafood should turn opaque throughout and firm.

BAKED FISH WITH HERBS AND LEMON

Serves 2 to 4

2 snapper or trout or any other
    whole fish, each 1 to 1½ lb

4 Tbsp olive oil

Marinade

2 lemons

4 cloves garlic, crushed, with a
    pinch of salt

2 ripe tomatoes, finely chopped

½ cup chopped parsley

1 Tbsp dried tarragon

1 Tbsp dried thyme

1 tsp chili flakes

1 tsp paprika

salt

From the age of seven until my early teens, once a month my father took my brothers and me to Akko, a seaside city in Israel. There was nothing else like the smell of the saltwater and the sounds of the waves as they touched my feet. We kids played on the beach and from time to time joined the adults. A waiter from a nearby restaurant would appear with a huge platter filled with freshly caught fish that he then grilled on a Hibachi in front of us. We sprinkled the fish with salt and lemon and snacked on it as we would nuts.

When buying whole fish, ask the fishmonger to clean both the cavity and the outside. Serve this dish with salad, olives and boiled potatoes or white rice.

1. Rinse the fish with cold water and pat dry with paper towel both inside and outside. Make a few cuts diagonally on one side of the fish. Set aside in a marinating dish, cut side up.

2. Squeeze the juice of the lemons into a bowl, reserving the lemon halves. Add the remaining marinade ingredients, stirring to combine.

3. Pour half of the marinade into the fish cavity and the other half over top the fish. Pop the squeezed lemons into the fish cavities. Drizzle the olive oil over the fish, then cover the fish and refrigerate for 1 to 2 hours.

4. In a deep ovenproof dish lined with parchment paper, bake the fish in its marinade in a 425°F oven for 45 to 60 minutes, basting after 20 minutes. The fish is cooked when it is brown and very tender, almost falling off the bone, and the skin is somewhat shrivelled.

5. To serve, cut just behind the gills down to the backbone, leaving the head intact. Turning the knife toward the tail, slice horizontally from head to tail (parallel to the backbone), leaving the skin on. Transfer the top half to a serving platter. Carefully remove the head and bones from the bottom half (you may want to use small needle-nose pliers to remove the small pin bones) and arrange that half on the platter. Drizzle the marinade over top both fillets.

At Akko, Israel, 2012

VARIATION

Instead of baking, barbecue the fish and use the marinade as a dressing.

In a bowl, combine the marinade ingredients. Rinse the fish, pat dry with paper towel and rub with olive oil. Barbecue over medium-high heat for 20 to 30 minutes per side, until brown and very tender, and the skin is somewhat shrivelled. To serve, slice as directed in recipe and arrange on a serving plate. Drizzle the dressing over top.

HERBED FISH PATTIES
ARUK BEL SAMAK

This recipe is dedicated to the memory of my late aunt Gitrout. When I first immigrated to Canada, I found odd jobs in factories and restaurants, and cleaning houses. I lived in rooming houses not always in the best condition. But still, I was better off than being an illegal immigrant in Europe. Gitrout was a distant relative who lived in New York. She would invite me to stay with her for a few days at a time, buying me clothes and cooking some of my favourite dishes. One of the dishes was *aruk bel laham*, potato patties filled with meat, and *aruk bel samak*, or fish patties. She always made enough for me to take some back home.

I serve this dish with a green salad.

1. Process the fish, onions, herbs and spices in the food processor until smooth. Transfer to a deep bowl.
2. Using your hands, squeeze any excess water out of the rice; mix with the fish. Using your hands constantly moistened with cold water, shape the fish mixture into patties slightly bigger than golf balls. Place on a baking sheet lined with waxed paper and chill in the freezer for 60 minutes.
3. Fill a large pot with water. Add the broth ingredients and bring to a boil.
4. Very gently drop the fish patties in one by one, being careful not to overcrowd them. Cook on medium-low heat for 30 minutes, then reduce the heat and simmer for 10 minutes.
5. Using a spatula, very gently transfer the fish patties to a serving plate. Carefully drain any juices from the serving plate before serving.

VARIATION

After the fish patties have cooled, heat some oil in a deep frying pan and fry the patties until golden brown.

Serves 6 to 8

2 lb fresh sole, halibut or haddock fillets (deboned)

1 large onion, finely chopped

1 bunch green onions, finely chopped

½ bunch each coriander, parsley and dill, finely chopped

1 Tbsp each cumin and pepper

1 tsp each turmeric and ground cumin seeds

salt

1 cup long-grain white rice, soaked in cold water for 1 hour, then drained

Broth

1 large onion (whole)

2 cubes chicken or vegetable bouillon

1 tsp turmeric

FISH FILLETS WITH RICE, YOGURT AND DILL

Serves 4 to 6

1½ cups Saffron Rice (page 76)

5 Tbsp butter

1 onion, chopped

1 bunch green onions, chopped

2 lb frozen or fresh haddock,
    cod, sole or whitefish fillets,
    sliced into strips

1 Tbsp cumin

salt and pepper

1 bunch fresh dill, chopped

2 cups plain yogurt

One of my philosophy professors at Queen's University in Kingston, Ontario, was active in social justice issues, including the anti-apartheid movement, a movement in which I too was involved. He frequently invited students and other professors to his home for a glass of wine or dinner, and he often made this fish dish. I think I went to heaven and back whenever I ate it. I serve it with a green salad.

1. Prepare the Saffron Rice.
2. Meanwhile, heat half of the butter in a large frying pan over low heat. Add the cooking onion and sauté until light golden. Add the green onions and sauté for 2 to 3 minutes.
3. Increase the heat to medium-low and add the fish strips, cumin, salt and pepper. Sauté for a few minutes. Add the dill when the fish starts to release its liquid.
4. When the fish is opaque throughout, add the cooked rice, the remaining butter and the yogurt to the pan, stirring gently to mix well. Season with salt and pepper to taste. Warm through, then transfer to a plate and serve.

CODFISH WITH CABBAGE AND POTATOES
BACALAO

My friend Edwarda and her mother used to make this typical Portuguese dish almost every Friday, and while I was in university in Montreal, I had dinner at their home almost every week. Edwarda's other friends, who came from all over the world—Africa, the Caribbean, Latin America and the Middle East—joined us. The meal always began with soup, followed by the *bacalao*. We often talked to each other in a mix of Spanish, Portuguese, French and English, and our heated political discussions could go on for hours. While Edwarda was engrossed in conversation, smoking her Gitane cigarettes and forgetting to eat, her mom made sure that the rest of us ate well. She explained to me that *bacalao* is also a typical Brazilian dish. The only difference between the two is that Brazilians cook it in the oven, while the Portuguese cook it on the stovetop. This is my version. Serve with fresh cornbread, olives, extra olive oil for drizzling and slices of lemon.

1. Soak the codfish in cold water for 24 to 48 hours, changing the water often to remove the salt. Drain.
2. In a deep pot, sauté the onion and garlic in the oil until light golden. Add the drained fish, water and bouillon cubes and bring to a boil.
3. Reduce the heat and simmer for 15 to 20 minutes. When the fish starts to break apart, carefully transfer to a serving platter and keep warm in the oven.
4. Add the remaining vegetables to the cooking liquid, adding more bouillon for flavour if needed. Simmer until the vegetables are tender, about 20 to 25 minutes.
5. Arrange the vegetables on the platter beside the fish. Just before serving, drizzle olive oil and lemon juice over top.

Serves 4 to 6

2 lb dried codfish

1 large onion, chopped

1 head garlic, chopped

3 Tbsp oil

5 cups water (or enough to generously cover fish)

2 cubes fish, chicken or vegetable bouillon

4 potatoes, sliced, then halved

1 small cabbage, quartered

1 red pepper, sliced

1 bunch Swiss chard, chopped (stems included)

olive oil, for drizzling

lemon juice, for drizzling

SPICY FISH CASSEROLE WITH POTATOES AND ONIONS

Serves 6 to 8

Casserole

1 large onion, chopped

1 head garlic, chopped

3 potatoes, sliced into thin rounds

2 ripe tomatoes, finely chopped

2 celery stalks, finely chopped (leaves included)

1 red pepper, thinly sliced

½ small cabbage, thinly sliced

1 cup chopped parsley

½ cup black or green pitted olives (optional)

2 lb frozen (thawed) or fresh cod, halibut, haddock or whitefish fillets

4 Tbsp olive oil

Sauce

1½ cups water

½ cup red or white wine or fresh lemon juice

3 Tbsp rice vinegar

2 cubes vegetable or chicken bouillon, dissolved in a little hot water

1½ Tbsp curry powder

1 Tbsp pepper or 1 jalapeño pepper, chopped (remove seeds for less heat)

1 Tbsp paprika

1 Tbsp dried thyme or dried basil

1 Tbsp sugar (optional)

salt

I had been making a fish with cabbage dish for a few years and was ready to experiment with it a bit, so I added more spices and herbs to jazz it up. I made this dish many times for my family, friends and neighbours, and the verdict has always been "excellent." A perfect dish for the winter, it keeps well in the refrigerator for a couple of days. I serve it with cornbread.

1. In a bowl, combine the sauce ingredients; set aside.
2. In a large bowl, combine all the casserole ingredients except for the fish and olive oil.
3. Pour the sauce over the casserole mixture, stirring to mix. Spoon half of the mixture into a large, deep ovenproof dish, add the fish in a layer, then top with the remaining casserole mixture. Sprinkle with olive oil.
4. Bake in a 425°F oven for 1½ hours or until the potatoes and cabbage are tender. Halfway through cooking, check the flavouring, adding more spices, herbs or other ingredients to taste. You should be able to taste the lemon and a touch of the herbs.

LEMON AND CHILI TUNA

While I was going to university, I lived in a rooming house up the street from Chabad House, a centre for Lubavitchers, a group of extremely religious Jews. Chabad House was a way to appeal to Jewish university students by providing them affordable homemade meals, with the hope that these students would stay behind for a religious lecture or, better still, for prayers.

For me, the opening of such a centre down the street was a blessing. I could go there on Saturday for a free meal, and during the week I got a hot meal for less than a dollar. My favourite meal was served on Friday—breaded fried fish with mashed potatoes. I always kept my head down and just ate. Whenever anyone tried to start a conversation with me, I just smiled and nodded. Although going to the centre did not convert me to becoming a religious Jew, I am very grateful for the homemade meals.

Over the years I cultivated a more sophisticated taste for fish, and deep-fried fish is not the only type I enjoy. However, I find that people who are not so keen on fish often like tuna and swordfish, as both have a meaty texture and are not as delicate as other types. Serve this dish with rice.

1. In a bowl, combine the marinade ingredients.
2. Place the fish in a deep dish and coat with the marinade on both sides. Refrigerate, covered, for 1 to 2 hours.
3. Heat 2 Tbsp of the oil in a large frying pan. Sauté the onion and garlic until light golden.
4. Add the remaining ingredients, except for the fish and reserved 3 Tbsp oil. Cook over medium-low heat until tender, about 20 to 25 minutes. Transfer to a serving platter and put in the oven to keep warm.
5. In the same frying pan, heat the remaining 3 Tbsp oil over medium-high heat. Sauté the fish (reserving the marinade) for 8 to 10 minutes per side, until cooked through. Arrange on top of the vegetables.
6. Pour the marinade into the pan and reduce over medium-high heat for 4 to 6 minutes, then drizzle over the fish and vegetables.

Serves 4 to 6

4 tuna or swordfish steaks (medium thickness)

5 Tbsp olive oil

1 large sweet onion, thinly sliced

1 head garlic, chopped

1 bulb fennel, trimmed and sliced

1 leek, well rinsed, sliced

1 cube vegetable bouillon

salt and pepper

½ cup boiling water

Marinade

6 cloves garlic, crushed, with a pinch of salt

½ cup chopped parsley or coriander

1 large tomato, finely chopped

grated peel and juice of 2 lemons

2 Tbsp olive oil

1 tsp chili flakes

salt and pepper

GRILLED SARDINES

Serves 2 to 4 (3 to 4 sardines per person)

1 pkg frozen sardines (approx 10 to 12)

fresh lemon juice

During a family vacation in Portugal, I ate sardines on an almost daily basis. We stayed in Oja del Agua, a tiny one-street fishing village in the Algarve with a magnificent beach. Every night we dined at a local restaurant, and every night I ordered a plate of grilled freshly caught sardines, served with slices of lemons, olive oil, olives and cornbread. Now, in Toronto or Montreal, whenever I go to a Portuguese restaurant, guess what I order?

Sardines are delectable. They are inexpensive and simple to make, and nutritious and tasty just on their own—the only thing I add to cooked sardines is a dash of lemon juice. The only problem is that the house takes on a fishy odour when I cook sardines. My family has been known to lock me out of the house if I am planning to cook sardines inside, so I'm forced to grill them outside.

Serve with cornbread, salad and olives. The grilled sardines will keep in the refrigerator for at least 2 days.

1. Thaw the sardines in cold water, then rinse well. Using your fingers, gently remove the scales. If you wish, you can also remove the heads with a knife and discard. Pat the sardines dry with paper towel.
2. Grill in an ungreased grill tray over medium heat for 15 minutes per side or until they are dark brown, the skin is peeling off and they look as if they are about to fall apart. Or bake on a baking sheet lined with parchment paper in a 450°F oven for about 15 minutes per side or until they look like they are about to fall apart.
3. Just before serving, squeeze the lemon juice over top. Remove the heads (if not already removed), slice the sardines down the centre and remove the backbone. The tails are nice and crispy to eat.

My father (third from far right) with his musician friends, Israel, c. 1957

SWEET-AND-SOUR FISH AND EGGPLANT CASSEROLE

SALAUNA BEN BABANJAN

My dad loved this popular Iraqi fish casserole. At least once a month he and his friends gathered to play and listen to music, taking turns meeting at each other's houses. He had done this when he lived in Iraq and Iran, and he continued the tradition after moving to Israel. Among his friend were several musicians who improvised music that was similar to jazz. These men understood and appreciated traditional classical Arabic music. One played the *oud*, a stringed instrument similar to a lute, and a *qanun*, a stringed instrument similar to a harp. They were accompanied by a cellist and percussionists. My dad and his friends would stay up until the early hours of the morning listening, playing music, singing, eating and drinking *araak*, an anise-flavoured alcohol. When at our house, they almost always ate sweet-and-sour fish and eggplant casserole.

Serve with white rice and a side salad.

1. Slice the eggplants into rounds about 1½ inches thick. Place on a greased baking sheet and sprinkle with salt, pepper and olive oil. Bake for 20 minutes in a 400°F oven.
2. Meanwhile, rinse the fish and pat dry with paper towel.
3. Combine the casserole vegetables (excluding the eggplant), spices and sauce ingredients in 3 separate bowls respectively and set aside.
4. Pour half of the oil into a large, deep baking dish. Spread one-third of the vegetables on the bottom. Sprinkle with one-third of the spices and mix. Place the fish on top. Make another layer with one-third of the vegetables and one-third of the spices, mixing gently. Add the cooked eggplant and then the remaining vegetables.
5. In a separate bowl, combine the sauce and the remaining spice mixture. Adjust seasonings to taste—the mixture should have a strong flavour.
6. Pour the sauce over the casserole and sprinkle with the remaining oil. Using a fork, gently stir to coat the top layer of vegetables.
7. Bake in a 400°F oven for 1½ hours or until the fish is cooked through and the eggplant is very tender. Taste the sauce after about 30 minutes of cooking and adjust the seasonings to taste—you should be able to taste the lemon and spices, with a hint of sweetness.

VARIATION

Omit the eggplant. Prepare as directed in the recipe above, except the first layer consists of half of the vegetables and half of the spice mixture. Place the fish on top, then add the remaining vegetables. Mix the remaining spice mixture with the sauce and pour over top. Sprinkle with olive oil and bake in a 400°F oven for 1½ hours.

Serves 6

Casserole

2 small eggplants

salt, pepper and olive oil, for sprinkling

2 lb whitefish, cod or sole fillets, fresh or frozen (thawed)

2 large ripe tomatoes, chopped

1 large onion, chopped

1 head garlic, chopped

1 red or green pepper, chopped

1 celery stalk, chopped

1 cup chopped parsley

4 Tbsp oil

Spices

2 Tbsp each cumin and curry powder

1 Tbsp pepper

2 tsp turmeric

salt

Sauce

1 can (14 oz/398 mL) tomato sauce

1 cup boiling water

½ cup fresh lemon juice

2 Tbsp ketchup

1 Tbsp sugar

2 cubes vegetable or chicken bouillon

MAPLE BAKED SALMON

Serves 4 to 6

2 lb salmon fillet

Sauce

¼ cup soy sauce

¼ cup maple syrup

2 cloves garlic, crushed, with a pinch of salt (optional)

1 tsp pepper

Years ago when I was living in Ottawa, for a summer job I worked for an agency that recruited affluent women for volunteer work in the community. My job was to phone these women and present the various options: working in seniors' homes, or for Meals on Wheels, or with underprivileged children. The organizers liked me well enough to take me along to conferences and meetings.

On one occasion, I was invited for a Sunday brunch at a volunteer's home. I left the brunch early to meet my husband to see my all-time favourite movie, *The Godfather,* Parts One and Two—a mere six hours. As I was leaving, the woman of the house insisted I take some food with me. She poured into a shopping bag at least two pounds of lox; into another bag she crammed bagels and cakes.

As soon as the movie started, Bernie and I dug into the lox. But before long, the people behind us started to yell, "You are making us all sick! Get that fish out of here!" I thought we were going to start a riot there in the theatre.

While lox has a very strong smell, baked salmon does not, and especially not when marinated with soy sauce and syrup. I serve it with rice and salad.

1. Place the salmon in a baking dish lined with parchment paper.
2. Combine the sauce ingredients and pour over the fish. Bake in a 425°F oven for about 30 minutes, until the fish is cooked through and flakes easily when tested with a fork.

GEFILTE FISHLOAF

The first time I tasted gefilte fish was in Israel at the home of the parents of my brother's fiancée, Erella. We were there to celebrate his and Erella's engagement. Her parents were Polish, so already that created some tension, since as Iraqis living in Israel, we had never befriended a non-Iraqi, and Erella's parents had never befriended a non–Eastern European. To make things worse, my mother did not speak a word of Hebrew, which Erella's parents spoke, so communication was limited.

The first thing we noticed upon entering their home was that the dining room table was beautifully set. My dad turned to my brother and said in Arabic, "They put lots of knives, forks and plates on the table, but no food." Iraqis normally put pots of food on the table for everyone to serve themselves, so this set-up was unfamiliar to him.

The first thing we were served was an Eastern European delicacy consisting of a cow's leg that had been boiled for a long time to produce gelatin. Once the gelatin cooled, slices of hard-boiled egg were added to it. We looked at each other, wondering what it was. My mother decided it was white Jell-O with egg, and she wondered why we were being served dessert first.

We were then served gefilte fish. As Iraqis, we were accustomed to lots of spices and herbs in our food, so the fish tasted bland to us.

But after many years, I have come to love the subtle taste of gefilte fish. Often it is boiled; other times it is baked in the oven as a fishloaf, which is the way I make it, as it is fast and easy. You can eat it as a starter, or serve with a salad and bread or potatoes for a main course, either way accompanied by horseradish. The fishloaf will keep in the refrigerator for up to 2 days but does not freeze well.

1. In a food processor, process all the ingredients. The mixture should be quite firm and not too moist. (Add more matzo meal and water as needed.)
2. Scoop the mixture into a loaf pan lined with parchment paper and sprinkle with olive oil. Bake in a 425°F oven for 1¼ to 1½ hours, until firm and lightly browned.
3. Let cool before slicing.

Serves 6 to 8

2 lb fresh whitefish, pickerel or a combination (ask the fishmonger to grind)

2 eggs

1 large onion

2 cups grated carrot

5 Tbsp matzo meal or dried bread crumbs

5 Tbsp cold water

1 tsp each salt and pepper

SAUTÉED SHRIMP WITH HOT CHILI TOMATO SAUCE

Serves 6

1½ lb shrimp (in shells)

4 Tbsp olive oil

1 head garlic, chopped

1 bunch green onions, chopped

2 large ripe tomatoes, chopped

1 cup chopped parsley

1 tsp chili flakes

1 tsp paprika

salt

Lately I have been shopping for my produce at a quaint Italian grocery store, where the clientele is my dream come true: retired working-class Italians who like to exchange recipes and advise each other on how to cook this or that vegetable. Once, I asked a fellow shopper how she cooked artichokes and she gave me her recipe. I thanked her and moved on. In the next aisle over, a woman stopped me to say that I should not follow the other woman's recipe: they were neighbours and she knew for a fact that that woman did not know what she was talking about. Of course, she proceeded to give me another recipe.

After buying the produce, I go to buy fish a couple of doors down. It's a very serious fish store, with very serious clientele. Not once have I been there without bumping into three or four people of various nationalities and having each one of them claim to know the best way to cook the fish I just bought. When it comes to seafood, I listen carefully and experiment with some of those recipes. I have finally perfected a sauce that I use for seafood platters and shrimp.

Serve with bread and a salad. Try dipping the bread in the sauce—delicious!

1. Rinse the shrimp, pat dry with paper towel and set aside.
2. In a large frying pan over low heat, heat the oil; sauté the garlic until light golden.
3. Add the green onions, tomatoes, ¾ cup of the parsley and the spices. Stir to mix well. Cover and cook for 5 minutes.
4. Increase the heat to medium and gently stir in the shrimp. Cover and cook for 7 to 10 minutes or until the shrimp are opaque throughout. Transfer to a serving bowl and sprinkle with the remaining ¼ cup parsley.

SEAFOOD PLATTER

While I was living in Arequipa, Peru, my friend and I got to know one of the few non-Peruvians who lived in Arequipa, a forty-five-year-old German man who lived with his elderly parents. We were invited to his house a few times. His parents had cow bells in every room so that at any moment they could call for the maids.

At one of their dinner parties we were served seafood as the main course. Afterward, the mother asked us to adjourn to the living room, where her son would play a few German tunes on the piano for us. After a short while, I felt restless and left the room to wander around. I noticed that the dining room table had not been cleared. I slowly moved toward it, looking over my shoulder to make sure no one was watching. Then, as fast as I could, I dug the serving spoon into the seafood platter, then put it in my mouth. Heaven! ... Until I looked up and saw the mother standing there, staring at me. I couldn't get the spoon out of my mouth fast enough. Sheepishly, I put it down on the table and returned to the living room to listen to the German folksongs.

Use any type of seafood you like for this recipe; the combination here is a suggestion only. I serve this seafood platter with bread and sometimes a salad. We eat it out of bowls so we can dip the bread into the sauce. You can also serve it over noodles.

◈   ◈   ◈

1. In a deep large pot, heat the oil over low heat. Add the sausage, onion and garlic; sauté for 5 to 7 minutes.

2. Stir in the chopped tomatoes, green or red pepper and jalapeño pepper. Cook for 5 minutes.

3. Meanwhile, in a small bowl, combine the wine, vinegar and water. Add to the onion mixture, along with remaining sauce ingredients. Stir to mix well and increase the heat to medium-high. Bring the mixture to a boil and cook for 2 to 3 minutes.

4. Reduce the heat and simmer for at least 2 hours—the longer it cooks, the more flavourful the sauce. Taste often to check the flavouring, adding wine, water, spices or herbs a little at a time as needed.

5. Prepare the seafood as close to cooking time as possible. Rinse the seafood in cold water. Slice the calamari into thin rings and pat dry with paper towel. Scrub the mussels and clams under cold running water, discarding any that are open. Pull the mussel beards away from the shells with your fingers and discard. Refrigerate the seafood in an uncovered bowl until ready to use.

6. Just before serving, increase the heat to high and bring the sauce to a boil. Reduce the heat to medium-high and stir in the seafood. Cook, gently stirring the sauce with two large spoons, for 7 to 10 minutes or until the shrimp are opaque throughout and the shells of the mussels and clams have opened. Discard any mussels and clams that do not open.

Serves 4 to 6

1 lb clams

1 lb mussels

½ lb shrimp (in shells)

½ lb scallops

½ lb calamari

Sauce

4 Tbsp olive oil

8 oz chorizo, sliced (optional)

1 large sweet onion, chopped

1 head garlic, chopped

2 large ripe tomatoes, chopped

1 green or red pepper, chopped

1 jalapeño pepper, chopped (remove seeds for less heat)

1 cup white or red wine

¼ cup rice vinegar

¼ cup water

1 can (28 oz/796 mL) crushed tomatoes

1 bunch each fresh basil and parsley, chopped

1 cup chopped mushrooms (optional)

1 cup chopped black or green olives

7 bay leaves

2 cubes vegetable or chicken bouillon

2 Tbsp each dried oregano and dried thyme

2 tsp sugar

salt

PAELLA

Serves 6 to 8

5 Tbsp oil

1 large onion, chopped

1 head garlic, chopped

1 jalapeño pepper, chopped
    (remove seeds for less heat)

2 chicken thighs

8 oz chorizo, thinly sliced

2 Tbsp paprika

1 Tbsp pepper

salt

3 large ripe tomatoes, chopped

1 bunch parsley, chopped

1 each green and red pepper,
    thinly sliced

1 lb frozen peas (approx 2 cups)

1 can (19 oz/540 mL) tomato
    sauce

2 cubes chicken bouillon

⅛ tsp saffron threads, steeped
    in 2 Tbsp hot water

1 tsp turmeric

3 cups water, plus more as
    needed

20 mussels (in shells)

20 clams (in shells)

1 lb shrimp (in shells)

1 lb scallops, halved

2 cups long-grain white rice,
    soaked in cold water for
    1 hour, then drained

olive oil, for sprinkling

chili flakes, for sprinkling

lemon slices

Paella is a lovely dish to serve because of the mix of colours. When I think of paella, I think of sunny Spain. No matter how small a town, people are out and about, drinking, eating and visiting. My husband and I had our first European vacation together in Alejante, Spain, a small town by the sea.

After spending the day on the beach we went into town for dinner. We loved sitting at the outdoor restaurants, talking, watching people, listening to conversations and just feeling alive. That evening, Bernie and I had just been served our sangria and paella when a fight erupted at the table next to ours.

A father and his son, no older than twelve or thirteen, got up from their table. The father wanted to punish the boy for something, but the boy evaded his father. Within minutes the son was running between the tables, the father chasing after him. They took off down a narrow laneway. Most of us in the restaurant, including the waiters, left our food and followed them, cheering for the son and calling out directions on how to avoid his father. After a few minutes the father returned to the restaurant, looking defeated. The rest of us trailed after him and simultaneously raised our wine glasses, saluting the little boy, who was nowhere to be seen.

Even though our paella dish was not sizzling hot by the time we returned to our table, it still tasted delicious. This is a great dish to serve at a dinner party, accompanied by a salad. There is something very intimate about everyone being served from the same beautiful plate.

1. Heat 2 Tbsp of the oil in a paella pan or large, deep frying pan over low heat. Sauté the onion, garlic and jalapeño pepper until light golden.

2. Increase the heat to medium-low and add the chicken, sausage, paprika, pepper and salt. Sauté for 7 to 10 minutes.

3. Add the tomatoes, half of the parsley, the green and red peppers and peas. Cover and cook for 3 to 5 minutes.

4. Stir in the tomato sauce, bouillon cubes, saffron with its soaking water, turmeric and 3 cups water.

5. Cover the pan with a lid and bring the mixture to a boil. Reduce the heat and simmer for 30 minutes, stirring frequently, until the chicken is almost falling off the bone. After about 20 minutes, taste to make sure the sauce is flavourful, seasoning with salt, pepper and paprika as desired. Transfer the chicken to a plate and set aside.

6. Meanwhile, prepare the seafood (as close to cooking time as possible). Scrub the mussels and clams under cold running water, discarding any that are open. Pull the mussel beards from the shells with your fingers and discard. Rinse the mussels, clams, shrimp and scallops in a colander, then pat dry with paper towel. Refrigerate in a bowl, uncovered, until ready to use.

7. Add the rice and remaining 3 Tbsp oil to the pan. Pour in enough water to just cover the rice—the grains should be visible. Bring to a boil, reduce the heat to low and simmer, loosely covered, for 10 to 15 minutes. Taste the liquid, adding more spices as needed—the flavourings should be quite strong.

8. When the water is almost all absorbed and the rice is cooked, add the chicken and the seafood and gently stir the rice so that the various vegetables and seafood are visible. Sprinkle with olive oil and chili flakes. Cook, covered, over medium-high heat for 8 to 10 minutes or until the shrimp are opaque throughout and the mussels and clams open. Discard any that do not open.

9. Sprinkle with the remaining parsley and serve immediately. Bring the pan to the table with lemon slices, so everyone can serve themselves.

TUNA SALAD WITH FRESH FRUIT AND NUTS

My family loves this salad. My dearest friend and co-worker, Jane, used to invite me regularly to her aunt's house, where she lived. Her aunt was a big, warm, cuddly but no-nonsense woman. She always had tuna sandwiches, potato chips and ginger drinks ready for us. One Saturday the aunt invited me to join her and Jane at the movies. She, of course, brought along sandwiches, chips and drinks. But what I remember most about that day is the bus ride to the cinema.

Some teens on the bus were staring at me and making fun of me because I had severe acne. Jane's aunt went over to them, gave them a piece of her mind and made them apologize to me. You can only imagine how embarrassed I was. That was not all; she then made them move closer to us and took out the tuna sandwiches to share with them.

This vivid memory comes to me every time I make this salad, which is similar to the filling of Jane's aunt's tuna sandwiches. The salad is a full dinner if served with bread. My son claims it is a fruit salad with a bit of tuna.

1. Combine the salad ingredients in a deep bowl.
2. In a separate bowl, combine the dressing ingredients.
3. Pour the dressing over the salad. Toss and serve.

Serves 4

2 cans (6 oz/170 g each) tuna, drained

1 apple or pear (or ½ of each), cored and chopped

1 stalk celery, finely chopped

½ small sweet onion, finely chopped

1 cup walnuts, chopped (or to taste)

½ cup chopped parsley

½ cup chopped dried apricots (or to taste)

½ cup chopped black, green or mixed olives, or 3 dill pickles, chopped

Dressing

juice of 1 lemon

3 Tbsp olive oil

1 tsp pepper

salt

Traditionally, Iraqis don't complete a meal with a dessert. My dad, when he wanted to have something sweet after dinner, would eat a spoonful of homemade jam. With tea we would eat ka'kat, sometimes plain, sometimes filled with cheese or dates. But for special occasions, such as religious holidays, weddings and the birth of a male child, we made special sweets to share with friends, neighbours and relatives, from almond balls to ka'kat filled with crushed almonds and sugar.

My kids and husband, however, like to finish a meal with dessert, so I have become accustomed to having one or two on hand, for them and for friends and neighbours who drop by to visit. Here are a few of the desserts I make regularly.

DESSERTS AND BEVERAGES

Bread Rings

ALMOND BALLS
HADGI BADAM

Makes about 24

2 egg whites, gently beaten, plus more if needed for moisture

2 cups ground almonds

¾ cup sugar

1 tsp crushed cardamom seeds (shell pods) (optional)

1 tsp rosewater or other flower water or cinnamon

2 to 3 Tbsp pistachios or almonds, halved (optional)

This delightful dessert is surprisingly easy to make.

A week before my brother's wedding, there were daily activities leading up to the event. On one day, the bride, Erella, had to be shaved and sent to the *mikva* or public bath to be purified for her future husband. In the early afternoon, the bride sat in my house, surrounded by dozens of relatives and friends, while Nasrat, my neighbour, plucked Erella's eyebrows with a string. Then we all paraded with food and desserts, singing as we walked, to the *mikva*. Neighbours watched us with envy, some ululating as we passed—a common practice of Middle Eastern women during celebrations. At the *mikva*, the guests washed, ate, sang and danced around Erella. Erella removed her clothes nervously, and then Nasrat used her string to pull Erella's hair. After the "torture" session was over, it took Erella a while to relax and feel like eating. I, on the other hand, washed and went directly to the desserts, to eat one of my favourites—almond balls.

I have reduced the amount of sugar in this recipe from that traditionally used, because I often find them too sweet. Store in a container—though in my house they don't last long!

1. In a bowl and using your hands, combine all the ingredients except for the pistachio halves. Using the palms of your hands, shape the mixture into small balls. Place on a baking sheet lined with parchment paper.
2. Bake in a 350°F oven for about 12 minutes or until light golden.
3. Remove from the oven and let cool, then top each with a halved pistachio (if using).

IRAQI PUDDING
HALAWA BEHEEN

My aunt made this pudding for me and my cousins when we were kids. We all sat around her as she bent over the gas stove stirring the little frying pan full of pudding, patiently listening to her stories about growing up in Iraq. My aunt had six daughters and very little money, and this pudding would have been fairly inexpensive to make. We ate the pudding either with spoons or by dipping pieces of pita into it. It is simple to make. Just dig in with your spoon or spread over a piece of bread and enjoy.

◈　◈　◈

1. In a small bowl, combine the water, sugar and rosewater; set aside.
2. In a frying pan, heat the oil over high heat. Remove the pan from the heat for a few seconds, reducing the heat to medium-low, then return the pan to the heat. Add the flour, stirring continuously until light golden.
3. Gradually add the rosewater mixture to the flour, stirring continuously to prevent lumps. Mix until the water has evaporated and the pudding is a creamy consistency.
4. Transfer to a serving bowl and top with the pistachios.

Serves 4 to 6

1 cup water

¾ cup sugar

1 tsp rosewater or pure vanilla extract

4 Tbsp oil or butter

4 Tbsp all-purpose flour

2 to 3 Tbsp whole pistachios

BAKED SUMMER FRUIT

Serves 6

3 peaches, pitted and sliced

3 plums, pitted and sliced

2 large apples, cored and sliced

2 large pears, cored and sliced

½ cup blueberry or orange juice

6 Tbsp sugar

1 pint carton strawberries, blueberries, raspberries or other berries of your choice

When I was in university, I occasionally treated myself to lunch at a Polish restaurant, which had specials for 99¢ and $1.99. The specials consisted of a little salad that I used to say was made in 1880, served with a piece of schnitzel or sausage and mashed potatoes and peas. Dessert was fruit compote.

A few years ago when I was in Montreal, I decided to look for the restaurant. Lo and behold, it was still there, but bigger and fancier. I went in and ordered the special I used to order as a student.

This delicious light dessert is very healthy. Because the fruits are baked rather than simmered, they maintain their wonderful crunchiness. Feel free to substitute pears and apples for the peaches and plums if you like. Serve plain, or with plain yogurt or ice cream.

1. Combine all the ingredients except for the berries in a deep, ovenproof dish. Bake in a 375°F oven for 35 minutes.
2. Meanwhile, rinse the berries. Slice the strawberries, if using.
3. Remove the baked fruit from the oven and immediately stir in the berries. Let cool before serving (it is best if chilled for a couple of hours).

BISCOTTI

Years ago, I had a dinner party. We ate very well but after we had cleared the dishes, my friends and my husband started to complain, "How come there is never dessert?"

So while they drank their wine and coffee, I went to the kitchen and tried to put together a cake. I used every ingredient I thought a cake should have and that I had in the pantry. I also had a couple of tomatoes and half a can of tomato paste in the refrigerator that I wanted to use up, so I added them to the cake batter. The tomato paste, incidentally, was flavoured with onion, garlic and spices, but I didn't think anyone would notice.

An hour later there was something that resembled a cake on the table. Everyone was so happy, but before long they had begun to complain again. There was something strange about this cake, they said. "It has a familiar taste to it," my husband commented.

After that, I decided to never again bake a cake but rather to stick to baking Iraqi cookies or biscotti. Now it's a tradition that on Friday nights I make a batch of biscotti. They're simple, crunchy and not too rich. They are also easy to make and keep well. You can double this recipe and either freeze some of the biscotti or just store at room temperature—they won't last long!

1. In a large bowl, combine the eggs, sugar, oil, cinnamon and vanilla. Gradually stir in the flour, baking powder and salt.
2. Add the almonds and any optional ingredients, mixing with your hands if necessary to combine.
3. Refrigerate the dough for 1 hour.
4. Line a baking sheet (about 12 × 18 inches) with parchment paper. Using your fist, press the dough to spread it out evenly on the baking sheet. (Sprinkling a little flour on top of the dough will make it easier to spread out.)
5. Bake in a 375°F oven for 20 minutes or until golden.
6. Remove from the oven. Cut the biscotti in half lengthwise and then widthwise into 24 to 36 pieces (I prefer them on the small side). Sprinkle with fruit sugar. For softer biscotti, reduce the oven temperature to 300°F and bake for another 35 minutes. For crispier biscotti, turn off the heat and let the biscotti stand in the oven for another 1 hour or longer—I sometimes leave them for a couple of hours or even overnight.

Makes at least 2 dozen

2 eggs

1 cup sugar

¾ cup vegetable oil

1 Tbsp cinnamon or 1 tsp almond extract

2 tsp pure vanilla extract

2 cups all-purpose flour

2 tsp baking powder

½ tsp salt

½ cup slivered almonds

fruit sugar, for sprinkling

Optional

1 cup chocolate chips

½ cup crushed walnuts (instead of the slivered almonds)

½ cup unsweetened coconut flakes

½ cup raisins

DATE SYRUP WITH WALNUTS

Serves 4

½ cup crushed walnuts

¼ cup date syrup, plus more
to taste

**Variation: Date Syrup
with Tahini**

¼ cup tahini paste

4 Tbsp date syrup

This is a popular Iraqi-Jewish dessert at Passover. Dates are popular in the Middle East. When they are in season, we eat them like candy, just as is or pitted and stuffed with a walnut or almond. We dip them in yogurt, and make cookies with them and date syrup to use as one might maple syrup and jam, and to drizzle on toast, ice cream or yogurt.

My brother, in Israel, invited more than 120 people for a brunch to celebrate his daughter's wedding. His family served the typical Iraqi breakfast: hard-boiled eggs, fried eggs with herbs and spinach, various types of pickles and salads, fried eggplant, hummus, labne, cheese, bread and jams. After this humungous breakfast, we were served all kinds of homemade Iraqi desserts and fruits. Then, as soon as the tables had been cleared, fresh homemade cream—thick like Devon or clotted cream—and date syrup were brought out. The cream was served on a large serving plate. To watch them, you would have thought the guests hadn't eaten for at least twenty-four hours. Each person dug a spoon into the cream and then into the date syrup. They devoured all of it.

To eat, dip pita or a piece of romaine lettuce into it. The refreshing lettuce contrasts nicely with the sweet cream. You'll find date syrup at Middle Eastern stores.

◇　◇　◇

1. In a serving bowl, combine the walnuts and date syrup.

VARIATION: DATE SYRUP WITH TAHINI

This dessert is very sweet. We typically dip pieces of pita into it to eat.

1. In a serving bowl, combine the tahini and date syrup, stirring to mix well. If too thick, add 1 or 2 spoonfuls of water.

Bakers, Petah Tikva, Israel, 2012

DULCE DE LECHE

This sweet milk sauce tastes similar to caramel. It is especially popular in South America, and while Peruvians and Argentineans typically make it from scratch—a time-consuming endeavour—I use a much simpler method. It's fantastic spread on crêpes.

When I lived in Switzerland, on my days off I would buy sweetened condensed milk in a tube. I looked forward to sitting on a bench outdoors with no one ordering me around, just enjoying the sweet milk. But the first time I had dulce de leche was in Arequipa, Peru.

1 can (10 oz/300 mL) sweetened condensed milk

1 tsp pure vanilla extract

1. Place the unopened can of condensed milk in a large pot of boiling water. Boil for 2 hours, making sure that the can is always covered by the water.
2. Remove the can from the water and let cool for a few minutes.
3. Open the can and scoop the milk into a serving bowl. Stir in the vanilla.

BREAD RINGS
KA'KAT

Makes at least 3 dozen

1 pkg (¼ oz/7 g) active dry yeast

1 Tbsp sugar

1 cup lukewarm water, plus more as needed

5 cups all-purpose flour (or combination of whole-wheat and all-purpose)

1 egg

½ cup oil

3 Tbsp fennel seeds

½ tsp salt

Basic *ka'kat* are small plain cookies made of dough very similar to that used for *khubz*, a round Iraqi flatbread, and shaped like a bagel. Sometimes I add sugar to sweeten them. When I was growing up, having ka'kat at home was as necessary as having water. They are almost a comfort food and always accompany tea and coffee. Even now when I visit my brother, we without fail stay up until the early hours of the morning talking, drinking tea and eating ka'kat. The night of my niece's wedding, we returned home from the party very late, yet we could not go to bed before drinking tea and eating some ka'kat.

As soon as the ka'kat have cooled, I put them in a resealable bag and pop them into the freezer (for up to 6 months). To thaw, just leave out on the counter for 30 to 60 minutes. They will taste as if freshly baked.

1. In a large bowl, dissolve the yeast and sugar in the water; set aside for 5 to 10 minutes.
2. Add the flour. Stir in the same direction for at least 1 minute, to incorporate the flour, adding a little more lukewarm water at a time if needed.
3. Add the egg, oil, fennel seeds and salt, stirring well to incorporate.
4. Turn the dough out onto a lightly floured surface and knead until firm and elastic. If the dough is too dry, add more water, a little at a time.
5. Return the dough to the bowl, cover the bowl with a damp cloth and let the dough rise in a warm, draft-free place for 1 to 1½ hours.
6. Grease a baking sheet or line with parchment paper.
7. Take a small piece of dough about the size of a walnut. Roll it between the palms of your hands to lengthen into a cigar shape. Pinch together the ends to form a ring. Place on the baking sheet. Continue in this way until all the dough is used, being careful not to overcrowd on the baking sheet (baking in batches if necessary), as the rings expand during baking.
8. Bake the rings in a 375°F oven for about 20 minutes or until light brown.

VARIATIONS
Add 1 cup sugar and 2 Tbsp cinnamon (optional) and omit the fennel seeds.

As extra garnish, fill with nuts, ricotta cheese or pitted dates (see pages 147–49).

KA'KAT FILLED WITH DATES
KA'KAT BEL TAMUR

In Calcutta, I was told I must visit Nahoum's Bakery, in the city's largest market, where over a quarter of a million people shop daily. The bakery had been there for years and was supposed to be the best. Everyone and anyone I talked to on the streets of Calcutta had heard of Nahoum's Bakery, so you can imagine it was not difficult for me to find the place. Frankly, I was curious and puzzled, since the name sounded Iraqi.

At the bakery, an older man who was the spitting image of my dad was sitting by the cash. The owner was an Iraqi Jew whose grandfather had moved from Baghdad to Calcutta in the late 1900s. Nahoum was close to eighty years old and spoke fluent Arabic. But what surprised me most was that he was selling Iraqi desserts. I told him how surprised I was. He smiled and said, "I am an Iraqi and will remain one even though my parents and I were born in India."

I stayed in his bakery for a couple of hours, and we talked in Arabic, drank tea and ate *ka'kat* filled with dates. Each time a customer came in, he introduced me as his niece and I automatically called him *Jhalu*—Uncle.

The dough is the same as for plain ka'kat. You can make the dough with or without sugar—your choice (see the variations on page 146). Once cooled, the ka'kat can be frozen in a container or resealable bag for up to 6 months.

◈   ◈   ◈

NOTE: If you have any leftover dough, use it to make plain ka'kat.

1. Make the dough according to the recipe (Steps 1 to 5).
2. While the dough is rising, combine the dates, water and oil in the top of a double boiler. Cook over low heat until completely smooth, adding a little more water if the mixture becomes too thick.
3. Meanwhile, in a small bowl, beat the egg white. Place the sesame seeds in a shallow bowl.
4. Grease a baking sheet or line with parchment paper.
5. Take a piece of risen dough about the size of a golf ball in your hand and, using your finger, press a hole in the centre. Using a teaspoon, fill with the warm date mixture. Pinch the hole closed.
6. Dip one side of the ka'kat first in the egg white, then in the sesame seeds. Place on the baking sheet, sesame seed side up. Using a fork, press to flatten. Continue in this way until all the dough is used, being careful not to overcrowd on the baking sheet (baking in batches if necessary), as the ka'kat expand during baking.
7. Bake in a 375°F oven for about 20 minutes, until light brown.

Makes at least 3 dozen

1 batch ka'kat dough (page 146)

Filling
2 cups pitted dates
4 to 6 Tbsp water
2 to 3 Tbsp oil or butter
1 egg white
½ cup sesame seeds

Offerings at Nahoum's Bakery, Calcutta, 1998

KA'KAT FILLED WITH RICOTTA AND FETA CHEESE

KA'KAT BEL JIBEN

Makes at least 3 dozen

1 batch ka'kat dough (page 146)

Filling

1 egg, beaten well

1 cup ricotta cheese

1 cup crumbled feta cheese or grated Parmesan cheese

1 egg white

At the age of eleven, I was sent to a boarding school. I was lonely, had no friends and was scared—no, petrified—of the authorities. I was also doing poorly academically and I became the joke of the class. With all this anxiety, I cried myself to sleep every night and dreamed about running away. One night my dream came true when my dear oldest brother, David, unexpectedly came with his friends to visit me. He brought my favourite cookies, *ka'kat* filled with cheese.

They arrived late at night. So late, in fact, that they had to jump over the fence, whistle and call my name outside my bedroom window. The rest of the school was asleep. When I went to the window and saw my brother, I ran outside crying and begging him to take me home. Then I ran as fast as I could to bundle up my belongings in my bed sheet. As I ran downstairs, I woke up some of the teachers. They tried to stop me, but I pushed through and ran to my brother. All the way home I munched on the ka'kat with cheese.

The dough is the same as for plain ka'kat and it can be made with or without sugar (see variations on page 146). Once cooled, the ka'kat can be frozen in a container or resealable bag for up to 6 months.

NOTE: If you have any leftover dough, use it to make plain ka'kat.

1. Make the dough according to the recipe (Steps 1 to 5).
2. While the dough is rising, combine the eggs, ricotta and feta cheeses in a medium bowl.
3. In a small bowl, beat the egg white.
4. Grease a baking sheet or line with parchment paper.
5. Take a piece of risen dough about the size of a golf ball in your hand and, using your finger, press a hole in the centre. Using a teaspoon, fill with the cheese mixture. Pinch the hole closed.
6. Dip one side of the ka'kat in the egg white, then place, dipped side up, on the baking sheet. Press with a fork to flatten. Continue in this way until all the dough is used, being careful not to overcrowd on the baking sheet (baking in batches if necessary), as the ka'kat expand during baking.
7. Bake in a 375°F oven for about 20 minutes, until light brown.

KA'KAT FILLED WITH ALMOND
KA'KAT BEL LOZ

The dough is the same as for plain *ka'kat* and it can be made with or without sugar (see variations on page 146). Once cooled, the ka'kat can be frozen in a container or resealable bag for up to 6 months.

NOTE: If you have any leftover dough, use it to make plain ka'kat.

1. Make the dough according to the recipe (Steps 1 to 5).
2. While the dough is rising, combine the filling ingredients.
3. Grease a baking sheet or line with parchment paper.
4. Take a piece of the risen dough about the size of a golf ball in your hand and, using your finger, press a hole in the centre. Using a teaspoon, fill with the almond mixture. Pinch the hole closed and place on the baking sheet, pressing with a fork to flatten. Continue in this way until all the dough is used, being careful not to overcrowd on the baking sheet (baking in batches if necessary), as the ka'kat expand during baking.
5. Bake in a 375°F oven for about 20 minutes, until light brown.

Makes at least 3 dozen

1 batch ka'kat dough (page 146), omitting the fennel seeds

Filling

3 cups crushed almonds, or 2 cups crushed almonds and 1 cup crushed walnuts or pistachios

1 cup sugar

1 Tbsp ground cardamom

2 tsp rosewater or 1 Tbsp cinnamon

SPICY ROASTED ALMONDS

Makes about 2 cups

2 cups raw almonds

1 to 2 Tbsp olive oil

2 Tbsp maple syrup (optional)

pinch chili powder or to taste

pinch sea salt or to taste

When I was a child growing up in Israel, a close friend of the family and his wife had their fifth baby girl. They became the talk of the town. My mother believed the wife was cursed and had to ask the Devil for forgiveness. Friends and relatives of the family were busy praying for the new mother. My father was busy calculating how much it would cost the husband to get all five girls married. My aunts were looking at the brighter side and hoped that the newborn would have her mother's blue eyes. After the birth, my mother and the aunts baked *ka'kat* and roasted almonds and took them over to the family. I followed them. The husband was sitting on the veranda smoking, moping and threatening to leave his wife, who had punished him by giving him five daughters. The wife, on the other hand, was sitting in the house with her five girls, crying and apologizing.

The women passed messages between the husband and wife, hoping they would come to some compromise. During that trying negotiation period, close to five pounds of ka'kat, pounds of roasted almonds and dozens of cups of tea and coffee must have been consumed. I was the helper who served and cleaned up. For every ka'kat and almond I served, I ate one of each. Finally, the relatives appeased the husband by telling him that his wife would talk to the witch doctor and ask the Devil for forgiveness and that this might help her to have a boy the next time.

The almonds I served had only salt. But I like to jazz them up a bit. I roast them on the weekend as a treat.

1. In a bowl combine all the ingredients, stirring to mix well. Spread on a baking sheet lined with parchment paper.
2. Bake in a 350°F oven for 12 to 15 minutes, until golden brown. Let cool before serving.

SESAME CANDIES
SEMESMYAH

When I was growing up, aunts and neighbours would make desserts in our kitchen for special religious holidays. We kids delighted in testing the various treats. We had the job of taking plates filled with goodies to neighbours and relatives. We always returned with plates filled with goodies from the recipients. As we sampled the desserts, the plates were closely examined by my aunts and mother to see if the appropriate number of sweets had been reciprocated. Inevitably, someone would complain that this person or that person was too stingy or had used too few almonds or too little sugar—and so the wheels of gossip began.

Sesame candies and sesame cookies (page 152) are just a couple of the goodies found on those plates. In the Middle East, sesame candies are widely available at street vendors, corner stores and markets. They are much thicker and larger than they often are in North America and definitely not individually wrapped.

◈ ◈ ◈

1. In a pan, toast the sesame seeds for a few minutes over low heat, until light golden. Remove from the heat.
2. In a small pan over low heat, warm the honey and sugar, stirring until the consistency is smooth and thick. Remove from the heat and stir in the sesame seeds.
3. Pour the mixture onto a baking sheet lined with parchment paper. Let it cool. Cut the slab into approximately 2- × 2-inch squares.

Makes about 3 dozen

2 cups sesame seeds

3 Tbsp liquid honey

3 Tbsp sugar

SESAME COOKIES

Makes at least 2 dozen

1 egg

1 cup sesame seeds

½ cup all-purpose flour

½ cup sugar

¼ cup oil

1 tsp baking powder

You can make these cookies as crunchy or as soft as you like, depending on the thickness and the length of time you bake them. Once cooled, store in a resealable container at room temperature for up to 1 week, or in the freezer.

1. In a bowl, combine all the ingredients and beat to a paste.
2. Spread the mixture on a baking sheet lined with parchment paper. Cover with another piece of parchment paper. With a rolling pin, roll out the mixture to cover the baking sheet. Remove the top paper and discard.
3. Bake in a 350°F oven for 15 to 20 minutes, until the slab has risen slightly and is light golden. Remove from the oven and cut the slab while still hot into approximately 2- × 2-inch squares.

SPICED TEA
CHAI

The Arabic word for tea is "chai." Most people in the Middle East, including Iraqis and Iranians, drink *chai,* often in small glasses. Iraqis add cardamom to it, while Iranians brew it very strong in a samovar, then drink it with a sugar cube in their mouth to sweeten it. But traditionally, milk is not added. Since my stay in India, I enjoy drinking Indian *chai,* made with milk and lots of spices. Here's my recipe for it. If you find it too bitter, sweeten with sugar or honey, or add more warm milk.

1. Pour the water and milk into a pot.
2. Put the tea leaves and spices in a square of cheesecloth and tie into a bundle. Add to the liquid and bring to a boil.
3. Reduce the heat to low and simmer for 10 minutes.

Serves 4

4 cups water

4 cups milk

4 Tbsp black tea leaves

seeds from 6 cardamom pods, crushed

½ tsp grated ginger

½ tsp cinnamon

½ tsp cloves

½ tsp allspice

½ tsp nutmeg

MANGO SMOOTHIE

I had this mango drink frequently during my stay in India. It's very refreshing.

1. Put all the ingredients in the blender. In just a minute or so, you will have a perfect drink.

Serves 4

4 ripe mangoes, peeled, pitted and sliced

3 cups plain yogurt or 1½ cups plain yogurt and 1½ cups milk

1 Tbsp sugar (optional)

1 tsp cinnamon

1 tsp nutmeg

Outside Calcutta, 1998

COOKING TIPS

Here are a few pointers to keep in mind when making the recipes:

◈ I suggest buying your spices in quantity—you'll use them up quickly with these recipes. I store some on my pantry shelf and the remainder in resealable bags in the freezer so that they stay fresh.

◈ To store lettuce and fresh herbs in the refrigerator for more than a day or two, first dry them on the counter, out of their bags. Then cover them tightly with paper towel or a tea towel and store them in plastic bags in the refrigerator. Rinse just before using.

◈ Many of the recipes call for chicken or vegetable bouillon cubes. I usually simply toss the cubes into the pot and let them dissolve gradually while the dish cooks. If you like, you can chop up the cubes before adding them to the pot. Or you can use chicken or vegetable broth, or substitute water, for the bouillon; just adjust the amount of water the recipe calls for accordingly. In general, chicken broth has less sodium than stock from cubes.

◈ I use oil, often olive oil, to sauté onions, garlic and other vegetables, rather than butter or vegetable oil. When olive oil isn't specified, any type of vegetable oil may be used.

◈ For recipes calling for crushed garlic, I crush the garlic with a pestle and mortar, adding a pinch of salt to it. I believe this is the best way to retain its flavour.

◈ When making a salad dressing, I add oil and lemon juice to the crushed garlic and let it stand for a few minutes—the longer the better.

◈ Warm lemons and limes in the microwave for 10 to 15 seconds on medium-high power before squeezing them. This helps release their juices. One medium lemon yields about 3 Tbsp juice, so for ½ cup fresh lemon juice you'll need about 3 lemons; for 1 cup, about 6. One medium lime yields about 2 Tbsp juice, so for ½ cup fresh lime juice, you'll need about 4 limes.

◈ Cooked dried legumes, usually beans, taste better than canned and contain less sodium. Soak them before cooking to reduce the cooking time. Once cooked, they are ready to use in the recipes. Always pick over legumes first to remove any small stones or grit, then rinse well.

Soak at room temperature in three to four times their volume of cold water for 8 hours or overnight, changing the water at least once. Drain and rinse.

Cooking legumes: Cook soaked legumes in a generous amount of water—about 3 cups for every 1 cup legumes. Add about 1 tsp salt per cup of legumes. Bring to a boil, then reduce the heat to medium-low and simmer, stirring occasionally and skimming off any foam from the surface, until tender. Chickpeas and kidney beans will take about 3 hours to soften; brown lentils, red lentils and black-eyed peas will cook in about 30 to 45 minutes. Once cooked, drain the legumes.

Yield: 1 cup dried legumes yields 2 to 2½ cups cooked. One 19-oz (540 mL) can of legumes equals 2 cups drained beans. Therefore, in recipes calling for a 19-oz (540 mL) can of beans or lentils, soak and cook 1 cup dried beans or lentils for an equivalent amount. However, in some recipes, the lentils don't need to be soaked and/or precooked; just follow the recipe instructions.

◈ Unlike with baking, determining the quantity of ingredients for these recipes was not a science, and you can change the quantities without adversely affecting the results. If the recipe calls for one eggplant and you have two in the refrigerator that you want to use up, use them both. If the recipe calls for a pound of meat and you have only half a pound, the recipe will still work, with only a slight adjustment in the quantity of the spices—or simply add more vegetables to make up for the lesser amount of meat. If the recipe calls for a pound of green beans but you have only half a pound, add other vegetables, such as carrots or celery, to make up the difference.

◈ The quantity of meat or poultry in the stews is relatively small, so you can use one or the other interchangeably without significantly altering the taste of the dish. If a recipe calls for meat without specifying what type, you can use beef or lamb or whichever type you like. When a recipe calls for a medium whole chicken, use one that weighs about 3 to 3½ pounds.

◈ I am very generous with the use of spices and herbs when I cook. For example, where some people might use one or two cloves of garlic, I often use a whole head. You can never ruin a stew dish by adding extra sautéed onions or garlic! Garlic and onion turn sweet when sautéed, and have a very gentle flavour. But with each of these dishes, you might want to start by adding a smaller quantity of the herbs, spices and lemon juice called for in the recipe. Gradually add more once the dish has cooked for a while and the flavours start to develop. Taste the dish constantly as it cooks and adjust seasonings to taste.

◈ I seldom specify the amount of salt, and sometimes pepper, used to season a dish. In these cases, add it to taste, but as with other spices, start with just a little at first—you can always add more. Often I indicate what flavours you should aim for in this or that recipe.

◈ Many of the stews start with sautéing onion and garlic. I sometimes cook two dishes at a time so that I have one dish prepared for the coming week. I have two pots on the stove and chop enough garlic, onion and meat or chicken for both dishes. Then I choose two vegetable recipes and follow the recipes accordingly. Any of the stews or poultry dishes can be frozen. To serve, thaw, then reheat on medium power in the microwave or for between 10 and 35 minutes or so in a 350°F oven.

RECITES LISTED BY PRIMARY INGREDIENT

ACKNOWLEDGEMENTS

There are a few people I must thank for their help and support: Cori Chong, who took the wonderful food photos. Valerie McDonald, who believed in this project even at its roughest stage. Akka Janssen, who brought to this project her expertise and her passion. Judy Phillips, who helped turn the manuscript into a beautiful book. And Peter Ross at Counterpunch, who is responsible for the book's elegant design.

ABOUT THE AUTHOR

Souad Sharabani, founder and director of Voice Print Educational Productions, is an independent radio-documentary producer, covering predominantly political, social and cultural topics. She has travelled, worked and lived on five continents and speaks five languages—English, French, Spanish, Arabic and Hebrew. For the past several years, she has spent her Mondays serving up nourishing, delicious meals to some 140 people in need through her volunteer work with the Parkdale Neighbourhood Church drop-in program.

Souad lives in Toronto, Canada, with her family and two dogs.

CPSIA information can be obtained
at www.ICGtesting.com
Printed in the USA
LVHW05s0844060618
579740LV00004B/4/P